Facing your nation

Discussions on Christian Responsibility in National Life

Editing and commentary by
William J. Krutza
and Philip P. Di Cicco

Contemporary Discussion Series

BAKER BOOK HOUSE
Grand Rapids, Michigan

This book is the result of the thinking of many Christian Americans. The bulk of the text in each discussion comes through their input. Sources are listed on the page of magazine permissions; for these permissions the authors are most grateful. Explanatory comments within the text, written by William J. Krutza and Philip P. Di Cicco, are in italics.

©1975 by Baker Book House Company

ISBN: 0-8010-5372-2

Printed in the United States of America

Contents

Foreword
by Senator Mark O. Hatfield

The Christian, like every citizen, cannot avoid being political in some sense. What he must do is bring the political realm of his life under the authority of Jesus Christ. Our politics must never be ruled by thoughtless conformity to our culture.

When we involve ourselves in discussions of Christianity and politics we often focus on how being a Christian is likely to make one a good citizen. This presumes that there is nearly a total affinity between the allegiance to Christ and loyalty to the State, particularly in a democracy. But this is not always the case as events of the late '60s and early '70s have shown.

For instance, during the period of debate in the United States Senate in 1970, when Senator George McGovern of South Dakota and I offered an amendment to end the Vietnam war, I received many letters from fellow Christians questioning my patriotism and personal faith. One of them said, "Why do you think you have the right to interfere with our President? Have you forgotten that God's way is to respect and honor those in authority? What higher power is there than President Nixon? God put him there. 'Whosoever, therefore, resisteth the power resisteth the ordinance of God.' " This appears to be an extreme example, but it prevailed at that time among many in the Christian community who concluded that faith in Christ meant that one should unquestioningly obey and agree with those in political authority. The resulting assumption, then, was that one need not involve his personal faith with politics.

The more I observe contemporary America, the more I read about the history of the church, and the more I study the scriptures, the more I sense the danger of merging our piety with patriotism.

We must recognize that our culture is not Christian in the truest sense of the word; therefore culture and Christianity cannot be equated. As a culture, we do not accept the ultimate authority of Jesus Christ over all people and nations and history. We do not all believe that our ultimate allegiance and trust must be placed in God's work of redemption and salvation.

It is significant that the title of this book is *Facing Your Nation.* Christians must acknowledge the fact that we are citizens of another world. Our ultimate allegiance is to Christ, not to Caesar. Hence the appropriateness of facing our nation rather than embracing it or condoning all of the activites of our government.

Much of the organized church of today, in my opinion, has allowed its thinking and its values to be conformed to the world. In subtle ways we allow our culture, with its civil religion, to determine our relationship to political power, instead of the scriptures and the relevation of Christ. The church today in many ways is the captive of our culture, and the religion of America is America. If we are to liberate the church and ourselves from the conformity to the world, then we must allow ourselves to hear the Word of God over the tumult of society.

Christians have a responsibility to model the love of Christ before their fellow man. In any given situation the details of this love may vary, but the mission of Christ as He described it in Luke 4:18-19 is to be worked out through His Body, the Church.

"The Spirit of the Lord is upon me, because he has anointed me to preach good news to the poor. He has sent me to proclaim release to the captives and recovering of sight to the blind, to set at liberty those who are oppressed, to proclaim the acceptable year of the Lord."

Christ's way was demonstrated to us in His ministry as being a way of love. He forsook both the extremes as they were represented by the Zealots and by the Sadducees. He condemned the Sadducees who were blind to injustice, and He resisted the Zealots who believed that injustice had to be met with violence. He proclaimed the way of love. His very physical force upon the cross was an exemplification of God's love. But His life also demonstrates that God's kingdom does not come through the world's means of political power. Rather, it must come through the power of love.

As we face our nation, both in its political and governmental activity, and in its moral and spiritual conduct, we will undoubtedly find ourselves at variance with trends in society and even with official policies. Unfortunately, as Christians we have too often either abdicated our prophetic responsibility or interpreted it in a narrow sense which excuses corporate activity and speaks only to matters of a personal nature.

Throughout history Christians have faced the nations in which they live. Sometimes they were in agreement with the conditions and policies of their nations. Often they were not. History has vindicated the activities of groups of believers who have fearlessly presented their witness. The blood of the martyrs, in fact, was the foundation of the Church. History has also revealed the hypocrisy of those who have not lifted the banner of Christ in the midst of injustice and those who even have used the power and appeal of the church to forward their own goals. The Crusades and the loud silence of the Church in pre-World War II Germany bear out this fact.

Naturally, we cannot approach this subject with reckless abandon. We must carefully determine if those issues about which we are concerned are vitally important and deserve the consideration of Christians who are in the midst of carrying out a mission begun and sustained by Christ. And if we do find it necessary to oppose established governments in some way, we must be ready to suffer the consequences of our actions.

Facing our nation is an activity that can result in praise and thankfulness for the liberties and opportunities we enjoy. It also can cause us to feel a frustration as we confront issues which seem to have no clear answers. We no longer live in a world of clearly defined issues. And as it becomes increasingly difficult to bear a living witness of the love of Christ toward our fellow men, the imperative of so doing becomes more urgent.

Today we need that kind of individual, and that kind of church, a confessing church, a body of people who confess Jesus as Lord and are prepared to live by their confession. Individual lives lived under the Lordship of Jesus Christ at this point in our history may well be at odds with values of our society, at odds with the abuses of political power, and at odds with cultural conformity in the Church. We need those who seek to honor the claims of their discipleship and to be continually transformed by Jesus Christ. Then we can be Christ's messengers of reconciliation and peace, giving our lives over to the power of His love, so that He might renew the face of the earth and of all humankind.

I trust that this book will be a helpful guide to Christians endeavoring to deal seriously with these issues.

Mark O. Hatfield
United States Senator, Oregon
October 1975

Introduction

The United States has always had deep religious roots. From the first Pilgrim immigrants to the circuit riders of the frontier, Americans have made their faith felt not only within the religious community itself but in the consciousness of the nation. Many of the earliest civil and national leaders were deeply religious men who looked upon their role of leadership as a calling of God.

Any examination of the early history of our country reveals that religion was not simply tolerated as a form of belief or used as a ritual. It was a vital element of day-to-day life. Though religious fervor ebbed and flowed, it would be hard to catagorize America as the *secular* country we view it today. The stamp of our religious heritage is written on our historical documents, our currency, and in our geography.

It is only in recent history that our religious heritage has been lost in a maze of secular interpretations of history and misguided applications of the doctrine of the separation of church and state. Actually, during the birth and infancy of our country evangelicals were at the forefront of social and economic reforms. Evangelicals were active in many forms of social reformation. They were abolitionists, prison reformers, founders of hospitals and schools, and so forth.

It was not until the rise of Fundamentalism that there arose a false dichotomy between social activism and religious practice. Fundamentalists, with strong reaction to the social evolutionary theories of the liberal churches and its strong eschatalogical leanings, concentrated on separation from the world and saving souls. They lost the balance between faith and works and became almost totally otherworldly, at least in their religious outlook. As a result of this emphasis the evangelical church lost its social momentum and for over fifty years hardly had a voice in the social and political affairs of this country. Then, when it did get involved, it supported measures that were grossly ineffective against social evils, as in the case of Prohibition.

Now many evangelicals want to change the situation. They see noninvolvement as a great heresy. They want to see the evangelical church rise to its true colors and become a vital force for *good* in the American social, economic, and political world. They are suspect of all theologies and ideologies that limit the work of Christians to saving souls from hell without caring also about the hell that is here now. These evangelicals want to return to the heritage of American Christians who were not only prophets, but pioneers of concern and patriots of involvement.

We can no longer stand aside in little individualistic cocoons while others determine the ethics and morality by which our children will live. Preaching against pornography and obscenity, for instance, will do little to rid our country of smut. But, conscientious Christians in positions of leadership and authority may very well be able to help put smut peddlers out of business.

Too often Christians have been on the questionable side of issues. In the past some Christians supported slavery on "Biblical" grounds. When they lost that one, they used the Bible to "prove" segregation. Today many Christians mindlessly attack anything they consider to be tinged with social activism. Yet many of these same people are the first to protest and take "action" when the issue touches their own ideological prejudices—such as busing, prayers in schools, and sex education.

Christians have a dual citizenship. As someone put it, they must walk with one foot in heaven and the other on the earth. This book concerns itself with the foot on earth. How we fare in heaven will depend largely on how well we act upon earth. We will be judged by "our works," according to Jesus. We will not be spared God's judgment if we claim to "save souls" here on earth while at the same time we fail to give the "cup of cold water" to those in need. We are not against "saving souls," but we are concerned that those who limit the gospel to preparation for life after death and the building of church memberships are preaching less than half of the gospel. Jesus ministered to the whole man. So should we.

We want Christians to *face their nation* because they are the "salt of the earth" and have the best resources to rebuild our nation in a time when it has lost spiritual and moral sensitivities. If any group can help this nation return to a high moral plane, it should be those who have dedicated themselves to the Lord of all nations!

Acknowledgments

For permissions granted by the following publications for materials used in this book, the authors are most grateful.

Permissions to Reprint:

Chapter:

1. "Revolution or Reformation: Which Heritage?" by Philip C. Bom from *Eternity* magazine, copyright 1971, The Evangelical Foundation, 1716 Spruce Street, Philadelphia, PA.

2. "Is the USA a Christian Nation?" by David O. Moberg from *Eternity* magazine, copyright 1968, 1716 Spruce Street, The Evangelical Foundation, Philadelphia, PA.

3. "A Politics of Love," an editorial from the July 1972 issue of *The Other Side*, Box 158, Savannah, OH.

4. "Jesus, Society and Politics," by Lane T. Dennis from the March-April 1974 issue of *The Other Side*, Box 158, Savannah, OH.

5. "Positive Politics" by Ronald Michaelson from *HIS* magazine, copyright 1972, Inter-Varsity Christian Fellowship, Downers Grove, IL.

6. "How Patriotic Should a Christian Be?" by Roger William Thomas from *Eternity* magazine, copyright 1974, The Evangelical Foundation, 1716 Spruce Street, Philadelphia, PA.

7. "Church and State: A Relation of Equity" by Nolan Harmon, from *Christianity Today*, copyright 1972, *Christianity Today*, 1014 Washington Building, Washington, D.C.

8. "What's a Christian Doing in Politics?" by Mark Hatfield from *Eternity* magazine, copyright 1968, The Evangelical Foundation, 1716 Spruce Street, Philadelphia, PA.

9. "What Are You Doing in Politics?" by Robert Shaw from *The Church Herald*, copyright 1974, *The Church Herald*, 630 Myrtle Street, NW, Grand Rapids, MI.

10. "Building Justice in the 70s" by Robert Linder, from *HIS* magazine, copyright 1972, Inter-Varsity Christian Fellowship, Downers Grove, IL.

11. "Two Sermons on War" one by E. H. Ammerman; one by Peter S. Lent from *Command* magazine, copyright 1975, Officers' Christian Fellowship, P.O. Box 36200, Denver, CO.

12. "The Destiny of America" by S. Maxwell Coder, from the January issue of *Moody Monthly*, copyright 1973, Moody Bible Institute, 820 No. La Salle, Chicago, IL.

1

Would You Sign the Declaration of Independence?

When this question was put to sixteen evangelical historians and other "experts" in an Eternity *magazine survey, there was a variety of answers. Twelve of the sixteen were qualified answers. Three gave unqualified "nos" and eight answered "probably no."* Eternity *commented:*

> *Issues that appear clear in retrospect may be anything but clear at the time of crisis. We admire the candid admission of some of our experts that they would probably have supported the Revolution even though they now see little Biblical justification for it; or that, while they hope they would have said No, they can't be sure. With the benefit of their hindsight, we are all alerted to the danger of being swept up in the mood of the hour, overconfidently believing that the Bible endorses our action.*
> *As Christians living in an age of unrest and change, we need to be sure we understand the Biblical teaching on the authority and function of the state, the quest for social justice and order, and the means of legitimate protest against evil. Classic New Testament passages include Romans 13:1-7; 1 Peter 2:13-17; Titus 3:1-2; and Matthew 5:38-42. Case studies to be found in the Old Testament include 2 Kings 9; 11:4-20; 1 Kings 18:1-16; Judges 3:12-30; and the*

compelling story of David's long and trying relationship with Saul.

With the full range of Biblical teaching in mind, we must judge the moods and fevers of our own time as carefully and dispassionately as possible, being especially wary of the crusader's temper. One of the most brilliant minds of the first century lived to regret his crusade against a sect called "Christians." When, by the grace of Christ, Paul was brought to his senses, he found that the Scriptures supported not his cause but the "enemy."

Philip C. Bom, professor of political science, discusses the question of revolution and reformation and how he feels Christians should respond to the issues that face American Christians today.

When the Pilgrim fathers landed on our shores in 1620 they came seeking freedom from religious tyranny. In 1776 our American founding fathers declared their freedom from the tyranny of an English monarch.

It is popularly thought that these two dates go together—that the principles cherished by the freedom-seeking Pilgrims contributed directly to the revolutionary struggle of our founding fathers.

But is this so? I do not think it is. I believe that if we want to discuss intelligently the religious and political foundations of America, we must distinguish between these dates.

In 150 years a great deal can happen to the religious direction of a people. The spirit of 1620 was different from the spirit of 1776. The difference was as fundamental as the difference between reformation and revolution. That is why it is necessary to distinguish between our forefathers (men of the Reformation) and our founding fathers (men of the Revolution). They were moved by entirely different spirits. A better understanding of the underlying principles of reformation versus those of revolution is critical for Christian citizens today. For in the confusion, disillusionment, and breakdown of basic institutions in our nation, revolution (and its spirit) is not the answer. Reformation is.

Who were our forefathers, the people who landed in New England? And what spirit guided their society? They were Protestants—men, women, and children of the Reformation. They took their stand against a corrupt Christian state and church. As C. Gregg Singer has written in *A Theological Interpretation of American History* (1964), they confessed the centrality of God's Word in all areas of life, in the world of labor and learning as well as of faith. They did not want to abandon education and economics to a "secular" sphere. God was to be honored in public service as well as in the worship service. They understood the distinction between church and state, but believed that both were instituted by God. The Mayflower Compact beautifully expressed this belief:

19

> Haveing undertaken, for the glorie of God,
> and advancements of the Christian faith
> and honour of our king and countrie . . .
> doe . . . in the presence of God, and one
> of another, covenant & combine ourselves
> togeather into a civill body politick; for
> our better ordering, & preservation &
> furtherance of the ends aforesaid; . . . and
> frame shuch just & equall lawes . . . con-
> stitutions, & offices . . . for the general
> good of the Colonie; unto which we prom-
> ise all due submission and obedience.

The Puritans who settled in Massachusetts
based their legal and moral principles on the
Judeo-Christian faith. In *A Body of Liberties,* a
legal document, forty-six of the forty-eight proposed laws were directly derived from the Old
Testament. Their hopes and dreams were rooted
in the Bible. They lived a God-centered life. One
of their basic principles was civil obedience ("all
due submission and obedience" to the laws they
had drawn up), an integration of freedom and
authority.

Unfortunately, the Puritans did tend to think
of themselves as a Chosen People, rather than
demonstrating the universality of the New
Covenant which Christ established for all mankind. But nevertheless, they showed in their
community life the relevance of the Word of
God to every area.

During the next 150 years, however, we
witness a gradual, but steady, spiritual and
political decline. At the time of the troubles

with England, revolutionary ideals were spreading rapidly through the colonies. In a letter to Hezekiah Niles, a Baltimore publisher, John Adams himself noted the change:

> The American Revolution was not a common Event. Its Effects and Consequences have already been Awful over a great Part of the Globe. And when and where are they to cease? . . . The Revolution was effected before the War commenced. The Revolution was in the Minds and Hearts of the People. A Change in their Religious Sentiments of their Duties and Obligations.

The change in the religious foundations of the political life of America is manifest in the principles of the Declaration of Independence: (1) that government is a human, not a divine contract; (2) that government exists to secure safety, freedom, and the pursuit of earthly happiness; (3) that when government becomes destructive of these goals, the people have the right to abolish it and establish a new form of government—a principle of civil disobedience.

The founding fathers were great politicians who made tremendous personal sacrifices. They were deeply religious men in the sense that they tended to deify nature, even referring to the Creator as the Great Legislator. As men of the Enlightenment, however, they proclaimed a natural rights rather than a supernatural rights doctrine. Their ideal of a republic was mainly rooted in the Graeco-Roman tradition of law and order. They were members of the "Party of

Humanity," not Christianity. Instead of acknowledging the centrality of the Word of God, they confessed to live by their own Reason, their "Oracle of Revelation." They believed in man's natural freedom, recognizing no higher or other authority than their own mind. They lived a man-centered life. Thus within 150 years a cultural transformation had taken place in this country. The former Christian colonies had become a humanist nation.

Thus, in addition to the separation of church and state, we also witness in our early national history the separation of Christianity from public life. Christianity was relegated to the private life only. Formal education was no longer considered the responsibility of Christian parents or the church, but was under the jurisdiction of the state. The public school still permitted prayer and Bible reading, but not Christian education. Philip C. Friese, in *Essay on Party* (1856), wrote that this separation of the "Kingdom of God from the republic of men" is at the heart of the American experiment in self-rule. Our form of government is historically known as republicanism, and wherever it has been tried—as in the French Revolution and its aftermath—republicanism has betrayed the stamp of dogged antisupernaturalism. This fact should at least put a brake on our uncritical acceptance of republicanism as a "Christian" institution.

It did not mean that the nation or the state's schools were without a religious foundation.

They were not. But it was Deism, a *natural* religion. And this same natural religion was the basis for a *natural* rights political perspective. Deism and republicanism were integrally related. As G. Adolph Koch in *Republican Religion* (1964) has shown, republicanism in politics was integrated with republicanism in religion. Both theology and politics followed the cult of reason.

WHEN CHURCH AND STATE ARE WED

The idea of separating church and state arose because too often in history when the two were wedded they deprived men of their freedoms and placed greater burdens on people than either might have done alone. History has shown that tyranny, corruption, and deceit often thrived when church and state shared inordinate power. Should we be hard on the founding fathers who wanted to keep America from inquisitions, popes, and witchhunts? Can we really argue with their wisdom? The United States has more religious freedom and greater church attendance than nations that presently have no sanctions against church-state alliances. In fact, citizens of those countries (such as the Scandinavian countries) with an alliance between church and state attend church less frequently and have less interest in religion than the people in the United States.

This has led, in our own time, to the rise of a political religion called "Americanism." Our public schools have generally been the instrument of the state for indoctrinating our citizens in this life-style, the so-called American-democratic way of life.

The evangelical response to this fruit of the cult of reason has been twofold. First, as a result of the early nineteenth-century revivals, evangelical Protestants defeated deism in theology, but at the same time accommodated themselves to it in politics. They appear to have accepted the disestablishment of church and state and the separation of Christianity from public life as one and the same development.

Second, by becoming increasingly concerned with saving individual souls and nurturing personal piety, evangelicals withdrew from the world and, in a sense, limited the message of salvation. They no longer believed—as had the Puritan Protestants—that all areas of life and all societal institutions should be submitted to the judgment of Christ.

Thus, indirectly, they may have contributed to the impression that the Bible is irrelevant to the social, economic, and political ills of our society. And directly, they may have contributed to the impression that the evangelicals support one religion in private, but another in public, namely, the American Way of Life. In the course of time, the two have been integrated in the popular mind so that for many they are synonymous: *Americanism* has become identified with *Christianity*.

Today America faces a fundamental crisis of confidence and direction. The affluent '50s made way for the over-confident '60s, which gave rise to despair in the '70s. At the 1970 annual convention of the American Psychiatric Association, Dr. Sheldon Wolin, one of America's most perceptive political theorists, said:

> The political life of the country is exhibiting unmistakable signs of derangement and systematic disorder. I would submit that the present crisis is the most profound one in our entire national history. . . . In contrast to previous crises, the present one finds the country not only divided, confused, embittered, frustrated, and enraged, but lacking the one vital element of self-confidence.

The crisis has affected liberals in particular because their political humanism, which has been dominant for the past two hundred years, is seriously questioned and found wanting.

The New Left and the Black Panthers wanted a new revolution, a radical humanism. Both justified their demands to abolish the political establishment by appealing to the principles embodied in the Declaration of Independence. They believed that the system no longer worked toward the ideal of life and liberty for all. They rebelled against Americanism, but maintained the tradition of revolution. Viewing the establishment as corrupt and tyrannical, they proposed to abolish it, just as the Declaration of Independence provides.

Ironically, the political establishment appeals to the same revolutionary ideals. During the 1968 campaign, Hubert Humphrey unceasingly reminded us that the ideals of the American Revolution are embodied in "the proud tradition of our party." And former President Richard Nixon, speaking as his party's standard-bearer in Miami, turned to the same source of inspiration to bring us together again. "My friends," he said,

> We live in an age of revolution in America and in the world. And to find the answers to our problems, let us turn to a revolution that will never grow old, the world's greatest continuing revolution, the American Revolution. . . . And so it is time to apply the lessons of the American Revolution to our present problems.

Thus our national leaders face the dilemma of condemning violence by taking inspiration from the same revolutionary principles as does the New Left! But was the Revolution really such a glorious, inspiring event?

In the glorification of our past, we often forget the immoral, destructive aspects of the American Revolution. It was a lengthy revolutionary war with all the inevitable evil consequences of disease, starvation, dislocation, and destruction of property. Estimates of American battle deaths alone range as high as 12,000 (proportionately, sixteen times the United States fatalities in Viet Nam). Out of a population of less than 3 million, approximately 100,000 Loyalists left the country as political refugees, their property confiscated.

After the War of Independence, the revolutionary leaders turned against each other, if not by terror tactics, at least by the stigma of treason. Dissent and opposition were considered subversive (Alien and Sedition Act of 1798). And the internal divisions were so deep that when the Jeffersonian Republicans gained preeminence, the Federalists seriously weighed the matter of secession, considering this a better option than supporting the Republicans (Hartford Convention of 1814). When all sides are considered, the patriots paid rather dearly for their Revolution, probably more than they had originally anticipated.

FREEDOM NEVER WON EASILY

On the other hand the revolutionary leaders showed a remarkable ability to build and unite a country that was torn by special interests. The remarkable result of their deliberations became the Constitution of the United States. It stands as one of the greatest political documents of all time. Freedom is never won easily. Surely the patriots paid dearly for their freedom. That is why they prized it so. The fact that a war had to be fought to gain political freedom and human rights does not mean these goals were unworthy. Many of the principles of the Revolution were based on humanistic values, yet many ministers supported the revolution and used their pulpits to fan the flame. Freedom, justice, and human dignity are not alien concepts in the Bible.

These facts reinforce the question of how

Christians can accept any appeal to the principles of revolution, whatever their source. As we have seen, revolution is the radical transformation of values, the substitution of humanistic for Christian values. As historian Carl Becker has carefully documented in *The Declaration of Independence* (1942), America tried to justify its rebellion by turning to the anti-Christian principles of the Enlightenment. And ever since then, humanistic values have permeated politics in America, in particular the political parties. Today there is danger that evangelicals will uncritically accept the appearance that we are in an age of revolution; that they will feel compelled to rededicate themselves to the meaning of the American Revolution, and apply its principles to our society.

But we must insist that revolutionary principles are not the answer. A society develops in accord with the religious direction of its people. Let us therefore break with the revolutionary principles of our founding fathers and rediscover the reformation principles of our forefathers.

Many of us have accepted the American Way of Life without a searching analysis of its foundations. It is one thing to believe in democracy as a form of government. It is quite another to believe in democracy as a social-political faith permeating all of life, all of man's institutions, including the church. This is what we have come to. The democratic way of life has become a political religion, like any other contemporary ism, and as such it is a real threat to Christianity. It is essential that we distinguish between Christianity and Americanism. Christ expects His followers to honor their nation-state, but not to glorify it on an untouchable pedestal.

Scripture does not demand that we defend the American Way of Life as over against the ideals of new revolutionaries. Evangelicals need not choose between these apparent alternatives; it is a false dilemma. Even the "American Way," inasmuch as it is man oriented, must lead to revolution. We should reject both the new and the old as revolutionary and humanistic. We should question, for example, one of the very basic articles of the American creed: that we are first of all Americans, irrespective of race or religion. We are Christians first, with our deepest and ultimate loyalties to Christ. Only after that are we Americans.

The only group of Americans who can hope to turn our country away from the inherent violence of revolution is our Christian minority. Christians are once again to become Pilgrims in America, a land estranged from God. With us lies the solution of reformation. By God's grace, we can avoid revolution.

But then we must rediscover the meaning of the Reformation and also understand the spirit of the times in which we live. To this end, we must better understand the demands of God's Word and Christ's command in the world.

Our big task, therefore, is twofold: (1) to provide a Christian political education, and (2) to witness for Christ in the nation. A Christian political education is necessary because Christians are deeply divided on principles, let alone on particular policies. There is no unity of thought, no Christian mind. In our discussions we are not really thinking *as Christians* about issues. We are thinking as conservatives or as liberals.

Furthermore, such education would emphasize the need for joint endeavor. For too long we have gone our separate, individualistic ways. The agony of Christians in America is that they do not constitute a political movement so they can stand together and encourage one another. Lacking unity, we cannot manifest the Body of Christ in the body politic.

Our options are not limited to joining some "activist" church or taking up a more vigorous, individualistic Christian witness. A more meaningful commitment for evangelical Christians would be to join a political-education organization. Such a movement could provide an avenue to effectively introduce a Christian perspective into the political debate and create an awareness of possible alternatives to reform the political structures. For instance, the need for a new Constitution is already being discussed. Are evangelical Christians going to let discussion and formulation of such a crucial document by-pass them and go to others by default?

We live in a troubled period of the nation's history. Yet it is a great time to be alive, with unprecedented opportunities for Christian witness. Americans, and evangelicals in particular, must rediscover the hope and vision of the men of the Reformation. Christians should be eager to participate in the public debate and confront the American people with the ultimate decisions they must make.

AGONIZING OVER THE ISSUES

Revolution as popularized by Leftist groups in modern America can hardly be equated with the revolutionary ideas of the founding fathers. Under ordinary circumstances most of the founding fathers would also have preferred reformation to revolution, but the times demanded the stronger medicine. The founding fathers did not believe in revolution per se, they justified it only in extreme cases, when the natural rights of men were at stake. They did not revolt over a few isolated misjudgments by the Crown; they revolted, among other things, to obtain the right to self-government and reasonable representation. They agonized over the issue before committing themselves.

Christians should take time to reexamine critically the foundations of our country. The standard of evaluation for evangelicals should no longer be whether something is American or un-American, but whether it is Christian or un-Christian. There is only one life-style acceptable for Christians in America, namely, Christianity as a way of life. Let us, therefore, reaffirm our Christian faith and choose for reformation.

The way of revolution is a way of death and destruction.

For Discussion

1. Can you cite Scripture verses that would endorse revolution as a way to change society and government? Does civil disobedience relate only to official barriers to preaching the gospel (Acts 4:18-20; 5:29-32) or does it have broader implications including revolution?

2. Based on the founding fathers' reasons to rebel against England, would you have sided with the colonists or with the Loyalists? Would you have signed the Declaration of Independence?

3. Because the founding fathers were "men of the Enlightenment" rather than evangelical in their outlook, does that mean we should disapprove of their actions against England or reject their political philosophy? Why or why not? Do you support political candidates today on the basis of their spiritual fervor?

4. Do you believe that the doctrine of the Declaration of Independence leaves the door open for the spirit of revolution such as has been advocated by New Left activists? Since such groups use the concept of the Declaration as their reason for rebellion, is that good reason for Christians to reject the idea? Why or why not?

5. How have Christians ignored the destruction and killing that attended the American Revolutionary War by glorifying the past and accepting Americanism and patriotism as sacred? What are the results of such Christian beliefs?

6. How did the American Revolution differ from the Russian Revolution? Was King George more corrupt than Czar Nicholas? Can we justify one and not the other? Can Christians accept any appeal to principles of revolution, whatever their source? Would it be disloyal to our country to reject the principles of independence and revolution implicit in the Declaration of Independence? Explain.

7. Why is it essential to distinguish between Christianity and Americanism? Does the Bible demand we defend the American Way of Life? What does Scripture say about supporting one's government?

8. In what ways does Evangelical concern for personal piety and saving souls contribute to the impression that the Bible is irrelevant to the social and political ills of our country?

9. Does "putting Christ first" in our lives mean that we have to reject our political heritage? Why or why not?

10. Why should Christians unite in their thinking on how political principles relate to the Scriptures? How has thinking as "conservatives" and "liberals" hurt our ability to unify as a vital Christian force in our nation?

2

Is the United States a Christian Nation?

Dr. David O. Moberg, chairman of the depart-
ment of sociology at Marquette University, gives
an answer to this question.

Beatle John Lennon once declared, "Christianity will go. It will vanish and shrink. . . . We're
more popular than Jesus now."

Scores of righteously indignant disc jockeys
declared that they would no longer broadcast
music by the Beatles. Acrimonious condemna-
tions of their antireligious spirit appeared in
numerous journals.

But was the criticism in America sharpened
by an unconscious feeling that Lennon may be
right? Is it not possible that Christianity *is* de-
clining here? Have we become a secular nation?
And what will happen to our national and personal freedom if God is no longer on our side?

Some will probably hasten to say: Didn't you
hear the great hue and cry over the Supreme
Court decisions banning prayer in the schools?
Didn't you follow Senator Everett Dirksen's gal-
lant fight to pass a "Prayer Amendment" to the
Constitution? And isn't there a "Christian
Amendment" movement aimed at official ac-
knowledgment of the Lordship of Christ over

the United States? This nation has never been more moral and "civilized" than it is today.

Who is right? Is the United States a Christian nation, or has it abdicated the privileges associated with such a title?

RELIGION IN EARLY AMERICA

In the first thirteen colonies, less than 10 percent of the people claimed allegiance to the church. Most of the country's leaders were not of evangelical persuasion. But as the country's frontier expanded, the rugged spirit of revivalism brought a greater percentage of the population into the church. Today an estimated 60 percent of the population is church related, although only about 40 percent attend church regularly. This hardly makes America a Christian nation. But it does tell us that America is a nation with a large percentage of its population claiming some religious affiliation.

Over a decade ago the Pledge of Allegiance was revised by the addition of the words "one Nation, under God."

IN GOD WE TRUST is inscribed on United States coins and several postage stamps. In 1955 it was added to currency, and in 1956 it was adopted by Congress, without floor debate and with no dissenting votes, as the national motto. The national anthem praises "the Pow'r that hath made and preserved us a nation!" A national holiday, Thanksgiving, officially recognizes gratitude to God.

Prayers are offered in national and state legislative halls. The Supreme Court of the United States opens each session with the supplication, "God save the United States and this Honorable Court." Several of its past decisions have declared that ours is not merely a religious but a Christian nation.

The nearly universal recognition of Sunday in state laws and in the practice of federal agencies sometimes creates hardships for Jews, Moslems, and even Seventh-Day Christians. Most property of religious organizations is exempt up to generous specified limits. Chaplains are hired by public institutions, including Congress and the armed forces. Church membership is popular and religious themes are widespread in American society.

In the midst of "religious prosperity," however, there are disturbing evidences of rank secularism.

The late C. Wright Mills of Columbia University criticized churches for slavishly accommodating their message to the spirit of the age, adapting when they should be denouncing, reacting instead of originating, imitating in place of setting forth new models of conduct and sensibility.

The morality of war dominates the spiritual life of Christians, said Professor Mills, so the church refuses to speak out against preparations for World War III and uses Christian morals as "cloaks of expedient interests" instead of as "ways of morally uncloaking" them.

From within the church as well has come a

long line of criticism. Secularism within the fold, the idolatry of bibliolatry, the false worship of man's reason, the frozenness of God's people, the backwardness of those who unduly treasure institutional vessels, apathy in the pews, the Madison Avenue mentality in the pulpit, the *Gospel Blimp* approach to evangelism, materialistic standards of success for church programs, and the irrelevance of traditional churches to twentieth-century life are strongly condemned, and many pleas for "a taste of new wine" are made.

Still others point to crime and juvenile delinquency, alcoholism, race riots, divorce, sexual promiscuity, and such other social problems as mental illness, suicide, and poverty. If America truly were a Christian nation, wouldn't these problems be less severe?

There also are numerous contradictory values current in American society. Thrift has been a traditional American virtue, but credit buying undermines it. "Free enterprise" is praised at the same time as we notice that the success of many came less from personal effort than from "knowing the right person" or taking advantage of special tax benefits and government handouts. Capitalism is praised as a great Christian economic system, but others condemn it as based upon self-seeking individualism and personal greed. Brotherly love is given lip service, but in love and war a kind of "dog-eat-dog" competition is praised for having made America great.

A Victorian sex code is still given lip service by many people, while sex appeal is used to sell everything from lamp shades to dog food. We are encouraged to get away with all we can on the basis of an unspoken moral perspective that the only thing wrong with unethical conduct is getting caught.

CHURCH NEVER UNITED

Except for strong opposition to the use of alcoholic beverages, the church in America has never been united in a common cause. Denominations split over the pre-Civil War slavery issues. Today there is considerable dissension about social issues. Where among American evangelical denominations can you find unanimity of thrust? Is it this splintering of ideas and efforts within the church that has severely limited its effectiveness in transforming society?

Cultural inconsistencies spill over into the churches. Many Christians are confused about their responsibilities in the world and their relationships to their fellowmen. They say, "The church's mission is not of this world, so the church should stick to the gospel of redemption and not get involved with social, economic, and political issues."

Others, however, read the Scriptures with more care. They find that Jesus addressed Himself very clearly to similar inconsistencies in His cultural setting, and most of all to those which had been incorporated into religious traditions. Picayunish details of sabbath-keeping had been stressed so much by the Pharisees that they did not recognize "the sabbath was made for man, and not man for the sabbath" (Mark 2:23-28). They forgot that "it is lawful to do good on the sabbath day" (Matt. 12:9-13). They were so busy measuring out tithes for their church that they overlooked more important matters of justice, mercy, and faith (Matt. 23:1-39). The Sermon on the Mount and the example of His life similarly revealed Christ's concern for practical action as well as abstract faith. As James later expressed it, "Faith without works is dead, being alone" (James 2:17).

If some Christians are right, the greater your other-worldliness, the greater is your sanctification. But others hold that as Christian values are applied in the world and woven into personal and group affairs, they pervade the national culture so that Christianity prevails. But with either definition the United States of America can hardly be called "Christian."

When scholars try to describe the chief characteristics of American society, the results are confusing. Americans are described as generous by some, but niggardly by others; as sympathetic, yet unfeeling; as idealistic, though cynical; as visionary, nevertheless practical. Part of the difficulty in analyzing the American character is the great diversity of its people. No single community, no group of people, no city or county is fully typical of all. "The American

Way of Life" means almost anything one wants it to mean.

It is obvious that Christianity is not a legally established national religion officially receiving special benefits denied to Judaism and other faiths. The separation of church and state is not, however, a sign that the gospel is inferior to government, as some Europeans might think. On the contrary, just the opposite may be the case. No theocratic link of church and government can be used to absolutize men's imperfect decisions. No pretense is made that the president or some other finite man plays the divine role of leading other men in the paths of God in national affairs. Yet there is a genuine national friendliness to the ethics of Christianity, if not to the Person of its Founder, Jesus Christ.

In the sense that all nations are under the will of God, the USSR and Communist China are as much "under God" as the United States is, for He is infinite, omnipotent, omniscient, and omnipresent. Transcending all the powers as well as all the limitations of human abilities, institutions, and nations, He is the Sovereign of the universe. As the Negro spiritual puts it, "He's got the whole world in His hands."

"CIVIL RELIGION"

A distinction must be made between true Christianity which submits to the Lordship of Jesus Christ and the authority of the Bible, . . . and what Senator Mark Hatfield refers to as "civil *religion." * Civil religion *centers in a worship of the office of the president, the popularization of God in governmental language, political acknowledgement of God through such activities as prayer breakfasts, pausing for prayer at football games, moments of silent prayer in memory of war dead, and other such practices.*

Nevertheless, the majority of men do not acknowledge His sovereignty. They are so tainted with unacknowledged and unconfessed sin that any nation which professes to be "Christian" can in fact be so only pretentiously and incompletely.

God's Word judges every human culture, including our own. Among other things, it teaches us that it is possible to have a "counterfeit faith," a "form of godliness" which denies the power of true religion (2 Tim. 3:2-9). There is an all-too-common belief that the American Way of Life represents a Christian culture which serves as a prototype for all other would-be Christian nations and that any deviation from traditional Americanism is un-Christian. This chauvinistic faith could have its source in the "angel of darkness" who comes disguised as an "angel of light" in his attempts to deceive even the elect of God (2 Cor. 11:14-15).

"They have heard that thou, O Lord, art in the midst of this people; for thou, O Lord, art seen face to face, and the cloud stands over them and thou goest before them, in a pillar of cloud by day and in a pillar of fire by night" (Num. 14:14).

"Blessed is the nation whose God is the Lord,
the people whom he has chosen as his heritage!"
(Ps. 33:12).

God is not a fetish to use like a good luck
charm in our purses, on our mail, in our pledge
of allegiance, and at public ceremonies. In order
to live consciously and consistently in a wholesome relationship with Him, man must make a
personal response to Him. The person who ac-
knowledges his own sinful imperfection, commits
himself to Jesus Christ, tries to live consistently
at all times (both in and out of church!) under
the guidance of the Holy Spirit, and recognizes
that he should not be conformed to the sinful
pressures of his society—this person lives "under
God" in the wholesome sense of that term,
whether his nation is commonly labeled "Christian" or not.

It is conceivable that the cultural forms of
American Christianity as we have known it may
go, as Beatle Lennon predicted, but God is not
dead and Jesus Christ remains the same, yester-
day, today, and forever.

For Discussion

1. On what basis was Israel a particularly religious nation? What distinguishing characteristics made it so?
Why didn't they guarantee its survival?

2. Can we transfer the theocratic concept of the Old
Testament into today's world? Has any nation succeeded
in doing this? What difficulties would we encounter in
attempting to do this?

3. How would one set up standards for establishing a Christian nation? How should these standards be enforced and applied? Would those who did not meet these standards be punished? On what basis?

4. In view of the divisions within the present Christian church, how would agreement be established as to which standards should be obeyed by the general population?

5. What are some of the dominant philosophies within the American society? Do these jibe with New Testament concepts?

6. What principles of our government do we generally recognize as having Christian origins? Do we think of our nation as Christian because the founders were Christians or because they used Christian principles when setting up its laws?

7. Why is it of value for Christians to recognize that our nation is not Christian? What is the danger of developing the concept of a "civil religion"?

8. In view of the specific command of the Great Commission of Jesus, is the effort to "Christianize" our nation a worthy goal?

9. How can we more effectively bring Christian concepts to the most crucial levels of government? How can these be made effective?

3

Can You Mix Love and Politics?

John Alexander, editor of The Other Side—*a magazine dedicated to applying Christian truths to America's social problems—talks about "A Politics of Love".*

As Christians approach politics, our point of orientation should be love. (In fact, *whatever* we approach, our point of orientation should be love.)

Hopefully this is not a point that needs to be demonstrated. Christ has told us that the first two commandments are love of God and love of our neighbor; the other commandments are commentary. And Paul tells us, "Faith, hope, and love endure, these three, but the greatest of these is love" (Williams).

But what is love? On a theoretical level this is a very difficult question, and many books have been written trying to answer it. But on a practical level the problem doesn't seem very difficult. You know what love is, and so do I. If a person is <u>hungry</u>, love is seeing to it that he gets food. If he lives where soldiers from one side invade his village one day and soldiers from the other side invade it the next, love is working for peace in that country. If a child is getting a poor education, then love is making it possible for that child to get a better education.

In short, love is being as concerned about the other fellow as you are about yourself ("Love your neighbor *as yourself*"). And "the other fellow" doesn't include just other Americans of your race and income bracket. It includes everyone.

LIVE BY GOLDEN RULE?

Some have ventured the idea that society would need far fewer laws and regulations if the majority of the country's citizens simply adopted the Golden Rule, "Do unto others what you want them to do unto you." Love is actively caring for your neighbor in at least the same sense one loves himself. Admittedly this is an idealistic concept, but it is so hard for even Christians to put it to work in our society.

So when we Christians try to decide what stand to take on an issue or how to vote, we'll think as much about the needs of others . . . as we do about our own needs.

What love provides us with in politics is a general orientation, not a detailed position on every question. Love gives us a mandate to feed people, but it doesn't tell us whether to do it by private charity, self-help, or government aid. Love means we work for peace, but is peace best achieved by appeasement or by mining ports? We must work for quality education, but love doesn't tell us whether that is best achieved by busing, private schools, federal aid to parochial education, or how.

In other words, love dictates the goals in politics, but it does not dictate the means (at least not as clearly). The best means are found by hardheaded analysis and experimentation, not by appeal to revelation. If a person is a Christian he will know he should be concerned about high unemployment, but he won't automatically know whether unemployment can best be decreased by tax cuts, government construction projects, or unbridled competition in an open market. This is a very complicated, technical question of economics which the Christian as such has no special competence to judge. That is a question which, like it or not, has to be left to experts.

DEFINING LOVE

Every person seems to have a personal definition of love which at times he does well in verbalizing. Often it contains considerable emotional qualities which are touching but quite unmeasurable. Demonstrative love goes beyond emotion (although emotion can't be eliminated because it is an integral part of every human personality) and involves intellect and will. These aspects of personality can be demonstrated in the political arena.

It may seem that if Christianity tells only what the goal is without dictating specific means, then it isn't of much use in politics. The hard thing may seem to be finding the means.

But that is not true. The hard thing is commitment to the goal of loving help for others. We would find ways to our goals if we were really committed to them. The present welfare system has not been astonishingly successful, but if Americans wanted to solve this problem we would experiment until we found a way that would work. What we lack is not the *means* to end poverty but the *desire* to end it. If we accepted the goal of ending racial discrimination, we could do it—but we won't. And the reason is not that we lack the means. The reason is that we have not accepted the goal which Christ has given us.

After all, when the Russians orbited Sputnik in full view of the whole world we didn't have the means to land on the moon. But in a few short years we found the means. We found the means because we accepted the goal of getting to the moon. Why did we accept the goal? Because the Russians had stung our pride, and we were afraid we might no longer be Number One in the world.

But hunger and racial discrimination do not sting our pride.

What would have happened if, instead of accepting the heathen goal of muscle show with the Russians, we had said to the world, "The Russians can have the moon if they want it. We will commit ourselves to finding protein sources, ending racism, and curing cancer. We think love of people is more important than winning contests of strength."

One of the chief reasons given for increasing American armaments is so that we can be the greatest power on earth. And we were told that we should support the SST so that Americans could continue to lead the world in aviation. One of De Gaulle's chief drives seems to have been the "glory of France." But such goals are hideously sub-Christian and will be rejected out of hand by anyone whose point of orientation is love. (Though, of course, we might still support building the SST, for example, as long as we don't support it for the sake of national prestige. We might support it, say, to provide jobs for those in the aerospace industry.)

Other goals incompatible with love also regularly appear in politics. In the '60s there was continual debate over whether property rights took priority over human rights. But this cannot be a question for Christians. For us, property rights are nothing compared to human rights. (Of course, this debate could be reformulated so that it involves two kinds of human rights, but the interesting thing is that advocates of property rights feel little need to reformulate their position.) Again it seems to be generally assumed that almost anything is good that will help the gross national product, but Christians must insist that the gross national product is not sacred. It should be encouraged to grow only if growth will, for example, provide jobs and decrease hunger without causing dangerous pollution and severely depleting natural resources.

Other non-Christian goals are also regularly invoked: the need to protect property values, the importance of not standing in the way of technology and progress, the necessity of generous foreign aid in order to protect our interests abroad, to name a few. So, clearly the question of goals is important. In politics it is not just that men of good will disagree over the means. It is that in politics, an awful lot of goals are not the result of good will.

This becomes even clearer if we get below the rhetoric and see what people really do in contrast to what they say. All politicians these days claim to have roughly the same goals, but their performance often makes their rhetoric look like a smoke screen to keep themselves looking respectable. For example, what about the man who says he is deeply concerned about quality education for black children but just happens to be opposed to busing? Well, if he is doing more to oppose busing than he is to get quality education for black children, then you can figure he's laying down a smoke screen. Or if he says he is opposed to busing because it violates local control but hasn't voted in a school board election for twenty years, then . . . Or if he says he wants to end poverty but is opposed to "welfare chiselers" cheating the government out of sixty-five dollars a week, then you must be very suspicious of him unless he is crying equally loudly about military contractors, income tax payers, and farmers cheating the government out of sixty-five thousand dollars a week. The disagreements are over goals more often than people are prepared to admit.

The importance of goals also comes out in the evaluation of established programs. Disconcertingly often programs originally established to help people become ends in themselves, and the programs become more important than the people they are supposed to help. Communism was originally intended to end the suffering of oppressed labor. But after Hungary and Czechoslovakia (if not long before), it is clear that hewing the party line has become far more important than preventing suffering. And liberals active in welfare often seem to be more interested in continuing an obviously inhuman welfare system than they are in helping the people that the system was designed to help.

One of the most important (and difficult) things for Christians to remember is that our goal is love and that any program is merely a means to that end. So we must remain flexible and have enough guts to abandon a program whenever a better means to our end is proposed. The absolute is love and if we become wedded to some program, we have forgotten what we are doing.

So, as the Christian approaches politics, all he really needs is to accept love as his point of orientation. The rest (the technical questions) will take care of themselves.

JESUS' LOVE DEMONSTRABLE

Since Jesus was extremely practical He never presented a concept that couldn't be demonstrated by concrete activities. His doctrine of love was not simply a hypothesis; it was demonstrable. Thus His command to love one's neighbor contains the idea that fulfilling His command will result in positive action toward others. He gives motivation to act. Demonstrating love at the community level is entering the arena of the politics of love. Christian political involvement in its simplest form fulfills the command of Christ to love one's neighbor.

The role of the church in politics is a difficult question. But the outlines of the answer should be clear. The church has special insight into certain areas (moral areas, the goals the state should pursue), and on these it has a duty to speak out. But in other areas which are technical and factual the church has no special competence. On these it has an obligation to keep silent.

There is a widely accepted dogma that the church should be silent about politics. But insofar as anything involves moral and spiritual issues, the church cannot possibly remain silent. That is true whether the moral issues arise in politics, personal lives, school, or wherever.

A denomination or minister which does not call on people to act in love is failing in its duty. The church must call on its members to be deeply concerned about poverty, war, suffering caused by alcohol, cigarettes, unsafe automobiles. It must call for repentance from those who are not concerned.

The task of the church in politics, then, is to make clear what the proper point of orientation is. It must condemn and call to repentance those who are concerned about national honor, GNP, progress, and self-interest rather than about love of people. In that way the church can help politics to be conducted in a proper Christian context.

LOVE AND POLITICAL PROCESSES

How extensively one applies love on a community level (be it local, state, national, or worldwide in scope) depends upon the depth of commitment first to Jesus Christ and secondly to helping needy people. Organized political processes, as slow as they are, still seem to be one of the best avenues to demonstrate the love of Christ. The political process gives Christians the challenge of making changes within their society based upon their concepts of Christian love. Christians can find may opportunities within the community to demonstrate the life-changing love of Jesus Christ.

The most important contribution of Christianity to an understanding of politics is its teaching on rebirth. Many think that the ultimate solution to man's problems is found in politics— if only we could establish socialism or a free enterprise system, everything would be okay. What we need, they believe, is some kind of political revolution.

But that is nonsense. What we need is transformed men, men who have new values, a new orientation, new motivation. No politics could produce a new man, but new men would produce new politics that would begin to end the suffering of humanity. "Therefore if anyone is in Christ, he is a new creation, the old has passed away, behold, the new has come" (2 Cor. 5:17).

CHRISTIANS INVOLVED

To say love can't mix with politics would necessitate many Christians already involved at all levels of government to give up their jobs. There are many senators, congressmen, governors, and state and city officials who first bow the knee to our Lord and Savior, Jesus Christ, before ever considering what they or we should "render unto Caesar." For such people in authority we ought to have the highest respect. To such people (regardless of political party or philosophy) we ought to give moral and spiritual support, letting them know in a most gracious and positive manner that we love them.

For Discussion

1. If you suddenly grasped the meaning of Christ's command to "love your neighbor as you love yourself," how could you initiate fulfillment of this command? Give some specifics within your community.

2. If love should influence the political processes, how can this best be shown? Be specific.

3. Can one ever become obnoxious or overbearing in his expressing of love in the political process? How?

4. How could a candidate for political office make love

of one's neighbor (spelled out in appropriate, constructive programs) the chief plank of his platform?

5. Why is there conflict between people on a political level even when both claim Christian love as their highest motivation? Is difference of opinion bad? Why or why not?

6. How different would your community be if true Christian love dominated political motivations?

7. What national policies would change if our overall political philosophy was dominated by love? Would it change our attitudes toward armament? Worldwide competition? The needs of the poor and the elderly? How?

8. Are there dangers in defining love too broadly? Does leniency of justice indicate the influence of love? Why or why not?

9. Why do political goals often clash with religious goals? Is love incompatible with political motivations?

4

How Would Jesus View American Society?

After years of silence, Christians have begun to pay attention to the Biblical implication of political involvement. Some of this concern came about as a reaction against political radicalism both in the United States and abroad. Some came through the challenges of the radicals who demanded better answers. Much of the new concern has been the desire to develop a clearer Biblical position, such as the approach of Lane T. Dennis, general manager of Good News Publishers, Westchester, Illinois.

A Christian response to social and political issues must be based on the gospel of Jesus Christ. This common starting point should result in some degree of atonement. But if we look to the church for direction, we see anything but agreement. There is rather a whole range of responses —from revolutionary to reactionary, from pietism to secularity, from noninvolvement to activism.

This lack of agreement seems to stem from a reluctance to seriously consider what the Word of God tells us about Jesus. Without this starting point Jesus may be made to represent whatever one wishes. But our right to claim Jesus' authority for our own position is legitimate only if it is based on who Jesus really was and what He said.

I stress the importance of the authority of the Word of God because of the all-too-common habit of speaking on social and political issues and claiming Jesus' authority without first trying to be clear about Jesus' attitude. Of course, when we are clear on what Jesus' attitude was, we then must ask how to apply that to our modern situation. Perhaps we will then adapt or even reject His attitude, but at least we must first see what His attitude was.

FACING ISSUES

The wide use of such books as Baker Book House's Facing the Issues *series has shown that many Christians are taking an interest in confronting the issues of our day in the light of the Bible. The* Facing the Issues *series covers fifty-two different issues designed to challenge Christians to face social, ethical, and moral issues with Biblical scrutiny, even though answers might not be easy to formulate or put into practice.*

The world comes to us with many "social solutions" that compromise evil rather than confront it. Some examples are the current permissive attitudes toward gambling, abortion, violence, and pornography. Christians must determine and assert their positions on these issues based on their understanding of Biblical principles and authority.

Jesus had much to say about the social injustice of His time. His first sermon was based on a text with the sharpest social implications: "The Spirit of the Lord is upon me, because he has anointed me to preach good news to the poor. He has sent me to proclaim release to the captives and recovering of sight to the blind, to set at liberty those who are oppressed, to proclaim the acceptable year of the Lord" (Luke 4:18-19). However the passage may be interpreted, there is a clear condemnation of social injustice implied in the text. Jesus saw His mission as being particularly relevant for the poor and the oppressed.

Jesus is no less outspoken on the problem of wealth. He uses the strongest language to warn: "Woe to you that are rich!" (Luke 6:24). But the poor are considered fortunate, for the kingdom of God is theirs (Luke 6:20). The rich young ruler who had kept the law asks, "What must I do to inherit eternal life?" and Jesus tells him, "You lack one thing; go sell what you have and give to the poor . . . and come, follow me" (Mark 10:17, 21). It may have been "only" a test, but it was a *real* one nonetheless. And how many of us would have passed it? Jesus clearly considered wealth an offense to the proclamation of the kingdom: "How hard it will be for those who have riches to enter the kingdom of God" (Mark 10:23).

Jesus did not accept social and religious ranking. According to social etiquette in Jesus' time, only certain persons would be included in the guest lists for important social events. But the people sitting at the table in the kingdom of God will be people off the streets and alleys, the poor, the crippled, the blind, and the lame (Luke 14:15-24). Social status likewise was considered by Jesus to be an offense to God's kingdom and intolerable where God's justice prevails.

When the woman in Bethany anointed Jesus' head with expensive perfume, those seeing the act were harshly critical—it could have been sold for more than three hundred dollars, and the money given to the poor! (cf. Mark 14:5). The ideological reasoning of Jesus' critics was rejected by Him. True justice is a deeper matter. Jesus suggests that if His critics were serious about justice for the poor, they should already have acted on this conviction in their own lives, rather than judging someone else.

Jesus was sharply outspoken on matters of social and economic injustice. But His view on these issues was not motivated by ideology. It was based rather in His single calling, to proclaim the kingdom of God (see, e.g., Luke 14:3; 9:2, etc.). In view of God's righteous kingdom, social and economic inequities are an offense to the will of the Father. So it is the priority of God's righteous kingdom which determines Jesus' attitude on all social issues.

Yet Jesus did not initiate or identify with a social reform movement. If we are honest about the Biblical text, we see that Jesus' actions were not directed toward the institutional level but rather were limited to the level of personal encounter. In the name of the kingdom of God, Jesus called people (rather than institutions) to repentance; He demanded individual change. The basis for social justice as proclaimed by Jesus was a fundamental commitment which altered one's relationship to God and to one's neighbor. Thus the norms of the kingdom which were the basis for Jesus' social radicalism, also became the norms of His followers.

Far from being above politics, Jesus' life was caught up in the political turmoil of His time. The world of the first-century Roman Empire was even more troubled than our own. Jesus' political attitude and activity must be understood against this backdrop. Palestine was conquered territory, occupied by the totalitarian forces of Rome. The Jews hated the Romans. They longed for liberation and reestablishment of the Jewish kingdom. In spite of the long history of foreign oppression, the Jewish people had not lost their hope that God would send His messiah to deliver them.

There were basically two types of messianic expectations. The first and most prevalent was that the messiah would come as a mighty warrior. He would lead a revolution and with God's help defeat the occupation forces and then establish a Jewish kingdom. This expectation was complete with an underground revolutionary group known as the Zealots.

The other expectation had its roots in the apocalyptic tradition, such as Qumran and the intertestamental apocalyptic literature. The messiah was envisioned by this group also as a mighty warrior, but his battle was of cosmic proportions. His coming would mark the end of the old age and the establishment of a new messianic age.

In view of the messianic expectations, Jesus' own messianic role was always in danger of being mistaken for something that it was not. Accordingly attempts have been made to see Jesus as a leader intent upon overthrowing the established order by revolution and setting up a Zealotist kingdom. There is considerable evidence that would suggest that many people did, in fact, mistake Jesus for a Zealot. One of Jesus' own disciples was a Zealot (Simon Zealotes) and two others may have been. Simon seems not to have lost his own Zealot hopes until after the resurrection. Further, Jesus' trial before Pilate was a political trial; the issue was whether Jesus was trying to become king. The inscription over the cross carried the Roman charge for which Jesus was crucified, namely being king of the Jews.

While it is clear from the Gospels that Jesus was not a political revolutionary, it is also clear that He was thought by many to be one. The point is that Jesus' life was not apolitical as some would like to believe. His life had far-reaching political significance, though not in terms of revolutionary activity or even in terms of "normal" political activity. It was based upon the kingdom of God which Jesus came to proclaim. The by-product of this proclamation was that

Jesus came into direct conflict with the established political order.

At the same time Jesus cannot be simplistically classed as being anti-establishment. His attitude was not based on a rigid ideology but was open also to those who represented the existing political order. Thus a (former) tax collector was included among the twelve, even though tax collectors were hated for their collaboration with the occupation forces.

The complexity of Jesus' political attitude can be seen most clearly in the question directed by the Herodians and the Pharisees to Jesus. In an attempt to tip His hand, they asked: "Is it right to pay taxes to Caesar or not?" (Matt. 22:17, NIV). But Jesus' answer would not allow simplistic ideological categories—"Give to Caesar what belongs to Caesar and to God what belongs to God" (Matt. 22:21, NIV). On the one hand He retained the critical attitude toward the established order; on the other hand He recognized the irrelevance of a question asked as a trick.

Everyone listening to Jesus was waiting to hear either an affirmation or a denial of his own ideology. But Jesus goes beyond ideology. He says that we give back to Caesar what in materialistic terms belongs to him—namely money. But we give to God what belongs exclusively to Him—namely our lives, which ultimately controls even what we do with our money.

On the one hand Jesus could not be part of the Zealot movement because it involved the establishment of a human kingdom brought into being by human effort. Both its means and goals were inconsistent with the kingdom of God which Jesus came to proclaim. On the other hand Jesus displayed unreserved criticism for the established order when it was in violation of God's kingdom.

Yet Jesus did not form a new political party or begin a political movement. If we are honest about the Biblical text, we see that Jesus' actions in political issues, as in social issues, were not directed toward the institutional level. They were limited to the level of personal encounter. In the name of the kingdom of God, Jesus challenged people rather than institutions. According to Jesus' own attitude and activity, the basis for political justice is a preceding commitment to the kingdom of God. That will lead to a new order in human relations.

TRANSFORMED FOR TODAY

The gospel changes people. Yet, change can't be kept strictly individualistic. When a person is transformed by the power of Jesus Christ, his new nature affects his immediate surroundings—such as his home, office, and community. Salvation has here-and-now dimensions as well as life-after-death assurances. Rewards in eternity will be based not upon the gift of God's transforming power in Christ, but upon our use of God's power that dwells within us. Thus our here-and-now actions and attitudes are the basis for our rewards. We shall be judged by our works.

The question now is: In what way are Jesus' attitudes and actions applicable today? Some degree of "translation" is surely necessary for we cannot simply transfer Jesus' attitude and actions into our own times.

It is argued by many that "translation" is impossible without some degree of adaptation. The argument goes that while Jesus may have been able to act only on the individual level in His times, our times are much more complex, calling for more sophisticated methods. That is, however, not altogether correct, for the milieu in Jesus' time was at least as gravely troubled as ours, and in many ways it was also similar to our own. There was social, economic, and racial injustice. There was religious and political corruption. There was a totalitarian superpower oppressing a captive people.

But in spite of this institutional and structural injustice, Jesus concentrated His efforts on the level of individual transformation rather than revolutionary change or political reform. With this in mind, it would seem that consistency with Jesus' attitude and actions in our own times would call for a similar response.

It is often argued that such an individual approach leads to a withdrawal from the world. But with Jesus quite the contrary is true. Jesus placed Himself in the midst of the turbulent social and political currents of His time. These currents pressed in upon Jesus from all sides and tried to force Him into their ideologies.

While rejecting them, He remained in dynamic tension with them until finally He was crucified for not giving His allegiance to the religious and political institutions of His day.

There is great pressure today from various ideologies to try to make the Christian conform to their values and methods. Revolutionaries call us to violence. Conservatives call us to maintain the status quo. Liberals call us to shallow reform. But Jesus calls us to seek the kingdom of God and in so doing calls ideology into question. When the world seeks to impose its norms upon us, the Christian who is consistent with Jesus' own ways will look to the Kingdom. It is at this point that the gospel of Jesus Christ becomes a scandal to the world and is offensive to those who view it from other values.

In many ways Jesus' attitudes and actions were "counter cultural." He called into question all that ran counter to the values of the Kingdom, and in so doing undermined their claims to ultimate validity. But I hesitate to say "counter culture" because this too has become an ideology which would claim ultimate allegiance. With this limitation in mind, however, the term is useful to describe the fundamental relation of Jesus toward all in His culture that ran counter to the values of the Kingdom. It describes a style of action.

From a historical perspective Jesus' emphasis upon individual transformation has not only changed people but all history. We see the radical implications already in the life of the early church (Acts 2:43-47; 4:32-35). But beyond this, Christianity, when it has been consistent with the Kingdom, has resulted in transformation of people and culture on every level. While the emphasis is upon the individual, if transformation does, in fact, take place it will affect every area of one's life. The evidence of such a transformation finds expression in all relationships, personal, social, and political.

We are not suggesting noninvolvement and political conservatism. Jesus' way is a call into the real battle—the only one worth fighting. And, as we see from Jesus and Christian casualties throughout history, it is a costly one. It is a call into self-sacrificial service for others, a kind of service which puts our lives—not just our ideology—on the line. It is a call to become personally involved in the lives of others: to feed the hungry, to house the homeless, to clothe the naked, to care for the sick and prisoner. We do this not to usher in the Kingdom, but to bear witness to the reality of the Kingdom and its power to bring the love of God into the lives of people.

Jesus' socio-political attitude and action are as radical today as they were two thousand years ago. Jesus calls all our ideologies into question as He did then. He calls us finally back to Him: to love Him, to love our neighbor, to "seek first the kingdom of God and his righteousness."

For Discussion

1. If Jesus walked the streets of your city, what do you think would be His main ministries? Would any of these have political implications or cause political conflicts?

2. Is it fair to criticize Jesus for not taking more "political action" in liberating the Jews from Roman rule? Was Jesus unpatriotic because He didn't resist Roman rule?

3. How significant, from the political viewpoint, was Jesus' emphasis upon transforming the individual? Would this supplant the necessity to transform political institutions? Why or why not?

4. By today's values would it appear that Jesus was copping out by challenging individuals instead of political institutions? How would His views be accepted by the political radicals of our day? By the conservatives?

5. Do you agree with Lane Dennis's emphasis that since political corruption and oppression are still evident in our day as in the time of Christ, He would still concentrate on transforming individuals rather than revolutionary social change?

6. In contrast to the totalitarian society under which Jesus lived, we have freedom to express political opinions contrary to our government. Would Jesus have been more open in His political pronouncements if He had had more freedom to speak? Why or why not?

7. How did Jesus view His mission on earth? Why is it important to take His mission into account when seeking to understand His political interest?

8. What does Jesus' attitude toward violence tell us about His political philosophy? Could Jesus be a political revolutionary in any sense with a philosophy of nonviolence?

9. What did Jesus mean when He said that the kingdom of God would be taken by violence? Does this have political implications?

10. Was Jesus' teaching on the kingdom of God political? Does the teaching in the Book of Revelation concerning the establishment of God's kingdom have political implications? If so, shouldn't our present view of God's kingdom also involve political values?

5

How Do You Make Your Vote Count?

In 1960 John F. Kennedy beat Richard Nixon by the narrowest margin in presidential election history. The count was so close that some Republicans wanted to have extensive recounts, especially in the state of Illinois where voting irregularities were taken for granted. Nixon did not press the issue, but many people became skeptical of the usefulness of their single vote when there was so much trickery going on. It is a standing joke in some large city elections to talk about the drunks who are driven around by party workers to cast their "votes" in the place of "dead men" in various precincts. (Somehow certain deceased individuals' names stay on the voting register long enough to be of some use.)

Some people call vote stealing "practical politics." In a sense that is true because it does assure their victories. But rather than becoming skeptical about the power of their vote, Christians need to remind themselves of the power of the ballot box. Honest elections have been won by the smallest of margins. Ronald Michaelson, a graduate of Wheaton College, served as assistant to former Governor Richard Ogilvie of Illinois. He encourages Christians to "positive politics" in a time when corruption and low morals among segments of our leadership have eroded confidence in government. He warns against becoming so disenchanted with the system that we become impotent to help it out of its own mire.

Unfortunately, a negative attitude is distressingly prevalent among evangelicals. For example, some Christians contend that since politics is so dirty it should be steadfastly avoided. It is ironic that these same people participate in the selection of our officeholders by exercising their voting rights. Yet by their attitude, they show little enthusiasm for reform of the political process.

British philosopher Edmund Burke said, "All that is necessary for evil to triumph is for good men to do nothing." John Stuart Mill, in his treatise *Representative Government*, asserted: "If we ask ourselves on what causes and conditions good government depends, we find that the principle one, which transcends all others, is the quality of the human beings composing the society over which government is exercised."

Our system of government is only as good as we want it to be, and evidently evangelical Christianity doesn't really want it to be very good.

If Christianity is the motivating factor in our lives, then it will affect our social relationships, our view of the political system, and our commitment to redeem the society in which we live. We will become involved—concerned about and dedicated to the principle of orderly change within our governmental process.

Opportunities for Christian involvement in political affairs are many—becoming a candidate for office, working on a campaign staff, working in a voter registration drive, or assuming a full-time position in public service.

Not all Christians can become involved to the extent described above. Nevertheless, through the responsible and informed exercise of the voting franchise, the Christian community can play a major role in the influence of policy at all levels of government.

What are some principles for the Christian voter?

First, cast your ballot on the basis of issues and do not allow personalities and other synthetic factors to dictate your vote.

This is very difficult to accomplish. The length of the ballot itself can tax the perseverance of the most dedicated voter as he attempts to carefully analyze the issues in each contested race. Efforts are underway to shorten ballots, but reform in the face of damaging vested interests will be slow in coming.

Quite often contests for lesser offices are not conducted on the basis of issues. For example, how often does one find a salient issue in the race for county clerk or trustee of the local sanitary district? Even some statewide offices do not evoke much issue interest in a campaign.

Political parties are not promoting issue-oriented campaigns for the simple reason that the electorate as a whole is not really interested in issues. We are in the era of the "new politics," where personal attractiveness, oratorical ability, potential appeal to various interest groups, and so-called charisma predominate as the party chooses its candidates.

Advertising in political campaigns reflects this alteration in campaign strategy. Television spots appeal to emotion, prejudice, humor, and loyalties while rarely speaking to the issues. When they do, distortion is usually the rule. In many campaigns TV stations refuse to accept "spot" political ads because they misrepresent rather than enlighten.

USE YOUR TALENTS

Christians with experience in the communication and media industries can put their talent and their Christian commitment to use by offering their service in producing and writing material for responsible candidates. Not all political activity involves door-to-door and people-to-people confrontation. Politicians need talent and they eventually get it, but if Christians do not "get into the act" they have no one to blame but themselves for underhanded tactics and gross misrepresentation.

Some argue that voting on the issues implies that the nonpolitical affiliations of a candidate are irrelevant. I believe that while the quality of a candidate's private life should concern us, it should not wholly determine our vote. Immoral or amoral public officials or candidates are certainly not desirable. On the other hand, Christians should maintain a broad-mindedness, rather than judge a candidate on some type of rigid, homemade code of ethics. Christ forgave, and we should be willing to do the same.

By the same token, a candidate's religious beliefs should be considered, but should not determine the way we cast our vote. We need to know a Mormon's stand on civil rights issues, a Quaker's position on war, and a Catholic's view of church-state relations. But when a candidate's religious posture completely dictates our vote, we exhibit a myopic view of the problems and potential in the world around us.

Finally, voting on issues might imply a corresponding neglect of political party affiliation. Although political parties are not mentioned in our Constitution, they have been a major factor in the continued viability of our democratic system of government. We must encourage the development of responsible as well as responsive political parties.

Parties vary from state to state. Due to regional configurations and the existence of coalition politics, one political scientist has suggested that we really operate under a system of four-party politics. Thus, while in one state party identification may be a valuable clue in ascertaining the issue posture of a candidate, it can be very misleading in another. The straight party ticket vote may be the easiest, but often is not the most responsible way for you to cast your vote.

Second, the Christian voter should avoid single-issue determinism. Although there may be a few exceptions, you usually shouldn't allow a candidate's stance on a single issue dictate your vote.

Many state governments have experimented with the concept of financial aid to nonpublic schools. This raises some constitutional issues related to the First Amendment.

Some evangelicals have vehemently resisted this concept, often without an adequate appreciation for the issues involved. While it doesn't follow that evangelical Christians should unanimously support aid to parochial schools, emotional opposition to a candidate or officeholder *solely* on the basis of his or her stance on this issue exhibits a narrow-mindedness that does not serve our system well. Informed and well-meaning Christians can oppose aid to parochial schools, but it should not become the sole determining factor when they stand in the voting booth.

Third, Christians have to learn to be content with less than an ideal candidate (unless you yourself are running!). It is highly unrealistic to expect to find candidates we agree with on every issue or whose personal character is unassailable. While we need not be confronted with voting for the lesser of two evils, we must understand that candidates for political office are mortal and have their own foibles. But they also have a potential for intellectual, emotional, and spiritual growth under the proper stimuli.

Finally, Christian voters should obtain the

most reliable information prior to voting. Newspapers, periodicals, radio, and television offer a wealth of information, but most have biases which must be recognized.

In recent years clergymen have become more active in promoting their positions on public issues. Religious propagandists have argued that the Bible unequivocally supports democracy, monarchy, socialism, pacifism, war, segregation, integration, and so on. Some fundamentalists behave as if conservative Christianity is necessarily married to a conservative political philosophy. This overly simplistic approach only serves to further alienate other Christians from participating in the mainstream of political thought and action.

On the other hand, it is often contended that there is no "Christian" or "evangelical" position on such critical issues as civil rights, poverty, welfare, the right to privacy, foreign aid, and urban renewal.

Shouldn't Christians develop their own viewpoint or perspective on these major issues confronting our country? Each of us must ask: What are the arguments on both sides? What are the consequences of choosing either alternative? Are any Biblical principles applicable? If so, what and how? We must take it upon ourselves to become informed and involved while at the same time respecting those, Christians and non-Christians alike, with whom we disagree.

One of the hardest parts of evangelical participation in politics is to remember that our society is pluralistic. It is not necessarily our task in the political arena to get everybody to accept our point of view. Politics can be a touchy process. It is easy to turn people off if we push our views upon them—especially our religious views. Some Christians violate their privilege to serve the public by proselyting at inopportune times and in misguided ways. They somehow have the idea they must "be a witness." They forget that they can do more good by simply doing good and saying nothing about it.

Eventually people will get to know you and will learn where you stand. Then they will be able to attribute your goodness to your commitment to Christ. But first they must see you do good. Your "testimony" can come afterward— naturally and spontaneously. Nothing is worse than forcing the religious issue at the wrong time.

If evangelical Christians resolved to become involved in our political system merely to the extent of exercising their franchise as described earlier, they could have a powerful impact on the processes of government. The assignment is not an easy one. It will take hard work, extra effort, tolerance, patience, understanding, and, above all, commitment.

History has shown that if a band of committed men who believe in a cause are joined together, things will happen. No successful revolution was ever conducted by half-hearted effort. Christians will never revolutionize our society, our system of government, or our sometimes misguided methods, unless we are truly committed to doing so.

Burke's observation of a few hundred years ago is timely now. Evil *will* triumph unless good men do something about it, and a good place for Christians to *start* is at the ballot box.

For Discussion

1. Why should Christians be concerned about the significance of their vote? How does the concept of the ballot box agree with the Christian principle of honesty and fairness?

2. Can Christians be more effective in showing the collective strength of their beliefs and moral principles by use of the ballot box? How?

3. What advantage would it be for Christians to organize themselves into voting blocks? Would it be contrary to their concept of government? Religious liberty?

4. In what sense can the corruption related to voting be blamed on the apathy of Christians?

5. Is the American concept of suffrage in keeping with Scriptural principles? Why or why not? Has general suffrage been good for American politics? Should anyone below age eighteen be denied the right to vote?

6. How does one become an intelligent voter? Why is it a Christian responsibility to be adequately informed on the beliefs and conduct of candidates?

7. How can the Christian community put "pressure" on political candidates to be sensitive to moral and spiritual principles? Why should Christians do this?

8. Should Christians affiliate with a particular political party? Why is party affiliation a good practical procedure? What is the advantage of being "independent"? What are the dangers of party affiliation?

9. How far should Christians go in proclaiming their faith in Christ within the political framework? What care should be taken against proselyting? Should Christians avoid using participation in political affairs as a means of proselyting?

10. How can Christians help "clean up" politics? How can you and your church start in your own community?

6

How Patriotic Should a Christian Be?

Students throughout the country, on small college campuses as well as at major universities, have challenged the accepted views of patriotism. Roger William Thomas, campus minister with Christian Campus House at the University of Missouri in Rolla, writes out of an understanding of the questions students ask.

The delicate balance between faithfulness to God and loyalty to one's country has always been a source of tension for Christians. This issue has become even more important as the American political system wrestles with one of its most serious crises in the two-hundred-year history of the republic. Today as never before Christians are being challenged to honestly evaluate the relationship of the faith to "the powers that be."

The beginning point for any Christian discussion of God and country must be the political ethic of Jesus: "Render . . . to Caesar the things that are Caesar's, and to God the things that are God's" (Matt. 22:17-25). The query that prompted Jesus' reply was of paramount importance to the citizens of first-century Palestine. Wrapped in that simple question about Rome's authority to tax was a whole bundle of sensitive political issues—issues surprisingly similar to those that confront us today.

For example, should a follower of Jesus support a corrupt political regime? Is patriotism a prerequisite to faith? What should the disciple's attitude be toward a government that conducts a systematic policy of oppression and involvement in the internal affairs of defenseless nations halfway around the world? Or toward a political-economic system that lives on the profits of war, or a system which overlooks leaders who are on the "take" from every vested interest in shouting distance?

What about taxes? Should a person willingly allow his money to be taken by such a government to spend on political crimes, human oppression, and international aggression? If he does, is he not participating in the evil?

Perhaps the first step toward understanding what Jesus taught is to note what He didn't say.

Jesus could have said, "Render to Caesar . . . period!" By such a statement He could have insisted that the ultimate authority is the authority of the state. Three centuries earlier Aristotle taught that the state was the ultimate social partnership that absorbs all other partnerships. Economics, education, and every other human pursuit was to be subordinate to the state. Thus, the purpose of education was to produce desirable citizens. To accomplish this, the state, not parents, were to control education. According to the philosopher's theory, private schools would be made illegal and everyone would be indoctrinated by the State Board of Education. Since no citizen would belong to himself, even the size of the family was to be determined by the state. The state was the ultimate authority.

Secondly, Jesus could have said, "Render to God . . . period!" He might have insisted that since God is the ultimate authority, no other authority really matters, especially if the rival authority happens to be a corrupt, pagan political system.

Such a view was popular in the Jewish culture of Jesus' day. First-century Palestine was an occupied territory. The Roman government had tampered outrageously with the Jewish religion and had wounded Jewish pride. The Palestinian hills were filled with rebellious Zealots with an unquenchable thirst for Roman blood. With swords flashing in the sun, the Jewish guerrillas would unleash their savage attacks on unsuspecting Roman garrisons screaming the cry, "No king but Yaweh!" When the Pharisees and Herodians (a pro-Rome Jewish political party) questioned Jesus concerning the tax issue, they were tempting Him to side with the Zealots in denouncing the authority of Caesar.

Jesus could have answered, "No king but Yaweh"—but He didn't!

Jesus could have insisted, "Render to Caesar because Caesar is God." He could have ratified the frequent claims of the Roman Caesars that they were divine beings due all the respect and reverence of a god.

The Caesar cult had begun when Julius Caesar was declared divine in 29 B.C. By the end of the first century, Domitian (A.D. 81-86) not only claimed divine honors but expected his subjects to refer to him as "Our Lord and God." First-century Christians were subjected to imperial wrath because they refused to acknowledge these divine claims.

Jesus could have said, "Caesar is Lord" — but He didn't!

Fourth, Jesus could have added, "Caesar is Caesar: God is God; and never the twain shall meet." He might have suggested a rigid separation of religion and politics that easily degenerates into a moral-less government. Such a view sees God and country as existing in two completely different worlds, allowing a people to claim to be godly while at the same time endorsing unethical activity for the sake of political expedience or national security. The pro-Rome parties *in Jewish society* came close to advocating such a policy. For them the most important issue was the preservation of a favorable political image in the eyes of the Roman leaders. Compromise knew no limits as long as it was profitable compromise.

Jesus could have sided with them by arguing that religion and politics don't mix, but He didn't. Caesar does have authority, but his is not the only authority. A follower of Jesus must render allegiance to his country, but that allegiance is not the ultimate loyalty. Caesar does have certain rights due him because he is king, but he is not free from God's authority. Caesar has his king, too!

JESUS AND POLITICAL ACTION

Some people have criticized Jesus for not taking political action during His ministry. But what is "political action"? Can we apply our understanding of politics to His times? Can we contend that His words and actions did not have profound effect on the political situation of His time and afterwards? And did not Jesus do a lot of things that we expect government to do for us today (such as taking care of the sick and feeding those who cannot feed themselves)? Some people call that "political action" today. Using that definition it is possible to say that Jesus did take "political action."

Jesus' political ethics form the foundation principles of the early Christian's response to the challenge of Caesar (Rom. 13; 1 Peter 2:13-17; Rev. 13–14). By understanding these basic truths, Christians can responsibly handle the tensions of the God-and-country dilemma.

The first truth that must control the Christian view of God and country is the unshakable conviction that *Jehovah God is the absolute sovereign of the universe.* All authority is subject to His authority. Jesus reminded Pilate of this during His trial. "Do you not know that I have power to release you, and power to crucify you?" warned Pilate. Jesus replied, "You would have no power over me unless it had been given you from above" (John 19:10-11). In the Old Testament, Daniel told Nebuchadnezzar that his kingdom had been given to him by the God of heaven (Dan 2:37). Daniel said of God that He deposes kings and sets them up. Paul referred to this same truth when he wrote, "There is no authority except from God, and those that exist have been instituted by God" (Rom. 13:1).

Jehovah is not a local deity whose sole interest is the preservation of one political system. He brings His judgment against wicked rulers and corrupt societies whether they claim to believe in Him or not (Amos 1–2).

The second truth is that a Christian's attitude toward his country must be governed by an understanding of the *Lordship of Jesus Christ.* During the second century A.D. the Christian community frequently found itself in conflict with the Roman government over this principle. Rome insisted that all patriotic citizens acknowledge Caesar as Lord and offer appropriate sacrifices of worship to the ruler. Countless believers were martyred because they insisted that Jesus alone was Lord.

There comes a point when the authority of Caesar must be held in subjection to the claims of the Lord of Glory. When that point is reached, a disciple must choose between obeying God or his country (cf. Acts 4:19). There will be times when it is a Christian's obligation to choose Jesus rather than Caesar.

At this point it is important to interpret

Romans 13 and Paul's call for obedience in the light of Revelation 13 and John's call for disobedience. In the first, government exists as a servant of God. In the other, the servant has become the beast. John describes a political power turned evil. The beast demands total allegiance and worship. What is the Christian response? Revelation 14:9-10 supplies the answer: "If anyone worships the beast and its image, and receives a mark on his forehead or on his hand, he also shall drink the wine of God's wrath, pure and unmixed into the cup of his anger, and he shall be tormented with fire and brimstone in the presence of the holy angels and in the presence of the Lamb."

Caesar's demand for worship and sacrifice is clearly an issue that involves the Lordship of Christ. What about other less obvious issues? Is Christ's Lordship also called into question when Caesar says, "Go to war!" and Jesus says, "Love!"? What happens when Caesar orders his subjects to kill, but Jesus says, "Feed your enemies!"? Whatever one's answer, Christians never forget that Jesus is Lord! The believer is never free to give unlimited loyalty to his government even in the name of patriotism.

Third, Christian patriotism must always be tempered by the knowledge that *the fellowship of the Spirit* is not limited by national boundaries. Paul's statement in Galatians 3:27-28 makes this unmistakably clear: "For as many of you as were baptized into Christ have put on Christ.

There is neither Jew nor Greek, there is neither slave nor free, there is neither male nor female; for you are all one in Christ Jesus."

The early critics of the Christian faith coined a phrase intended to discredit the followers of Jesus. Aristides and later Celsus labeled them a "third race." Christians were disloyal to both Greek and Jewish cultures. That label was quickly adopted by the Christians because to them it was a real insight into the nature of the faith. A Christian was a Christian brother no matter who he was or where he came from. Christians saw themselves apart from national or racial labels.

BLIND LOYALTY

This is a sticky issue when two nations are at war. Will Christians who are "patriotic" willingly fight for their country because they think they are right? It was not uncommon during World War II for Christian American soldiers to be fighting Christian German soldiers. Both may have looked upon themselves as doing a patriotic duty. But could both have been right? Was it possible for a German soldier not to know of the atrocities of the Nazis in prisoner of war camps? Perhaps the problem is having blind *loyalty to* any *cause. If we are truly devoted to the Lordship of Christ, we will not allow ourselves to become controlled by any human to such an extent that we condone or participate in evil.*

The New Testament presents a fourth truth that closely parallels this last one—namely, *the heavenly citizenship of the saints*. "Our commonwealth is in heaven," reads Philippians 3:20. The writer of Hebrews refers to the men of faith who saw themselves as strangers and exiles on the earth (Heb. 11:13-14). Christians are those who have no lasting city in this world (Heb. 13:14).

A beautiful Christian letter dated from the second century A.D. expresses this truth in a most marvelous way. A portion of the famous "Letter to Diogentus" reads:

> For Christians cannot be distinguished from the rest of the human race by country or language or customs. They do not live in cities of their own; they do not use a peculiar form of speech; they do not follow an eccentric manner of life. . . . Yet, although they live in Greek and barbarian cities alike, as each man's lot has been cast, and follow the customs of the country in clothing and food and other matters of daily living, at the same time they give proof of the remarkable and admittedly different constitution of their own commonwealth. They live in their own countries, but only as aliens. They have a share in everything as citizens, and endure everything as foreigners. Every foreign land is their fatherland, and yet for them every fatherland is a foreign land.

A Christian lives in both time and eternity and must share other men's concern over the problems of this world, but he must never allow these tensions to overshadow his faith and allegiance to Christ. A Christian should exercise responsibility as a citizen and should show appreciation for the tradition and heritage of his culture; but that appreciation must never become so strong that he forgets how to distinguish his Christian faith from his country's culture.

The fifth truth, one that helps explain God's purpose for governments, is the one most often forgotten—the sinfulness of men. Paul declares in Romans 3:23, "All have sinned and fall short of the glory of God."

This applies to American capitalists as well as Russian communists. Sin is not limited to certain tribes, races, or cultures. All have sinned!

Governments exist because God knows that sinful men must have controls or society will degenerate into total chaos. This is at the heart of Paul's understanding of Christian submission in Romans 13. "For rulers are not a terror to good works, but to the evil. Wilt thou then not be afraid of the power? Do that which is good, and thou shalt have praise of the same: for he is the minister of God to thee for good. But if thou do that which is evil, be afraid; for he beareth not the sword in vain; for he is the minister of God, a revenger to execute wrath upon him that doeth evil" (Rom. 13:3-4, KJV).

The refusal to acknowledge the sinfulness of men is at the heart of many contemporary political problems. The "liberal" politician whose views are governed by his humanist leanings is convinced that man is inherently good. And so, when much of the money and the well-intended programs end up lining the pockets of those who need it least, everyone asks, "Why?" Jeremiah knew: "The heart is deceitful above all things, and desperately corrupt" (Jer. 17:9).

Interestingly enough, the refusal to acknowledge the sinfulness of men is also basic to much "conservative" political theory.

Robert Welch, leader of the well-known John Birch Society, wrote a document outlining the Birch Society's views on opposing communism and socialism. One of the fundamental tenets of his entire political philosophy is the belief that "the government that governs least is the government that governs best." He insists that "the kind and quality of government is not as important as the quantity of government." Vital to this view of government is Welch's contention that man is inherently good. He calls this "the upward reach of man"—an evolutionary process. According to Welch, all you need to solve society's problems is for the government to get out of the way and let individual men go about their own business without governmental interference!

Both the liberal who thinks that sinful bureaucrats can solve all the world's problems and the conservative who thinks that individual sinners unrestrained or uninhibited by governmental control will prevent the problems are wrong! Because men are sinful God ordained governments to maintain order and justice. The question may not be how *much* government is good but how *good* is government.

In Romans 12 Paul explains the qualities that

make up the consistent Christian life. The tendency of most Christians to deal separately with Romans 12 and 13 explains much of the confusion concerning the interpretation and application of 13:1-7, for it is chapter 12 that sets the stage for chapter 13.

Several factors unmistakably mark the Christlike life. First, a follower of Jesus is a nonconformist (Rom. 12:2). He is willing to stand against the status quo. Francis Schaeffer says in *The Church at the End of the 20th Century,* "Christianity today is not conservative, but revolutionary.... If we want to be fair, we must teach the young to be revolutionaries, revolutionaries against the status quo."

Is there anything in a materialistic and militaristic culture more revolutionary than loving and feeding your enemy? (Rom. 12:20-21).

But a Christian must be more than a nonconformist. He must be a *transformed* nonconformist (Rom. 12:2). The only way a person can live a Christlike life is through the power of Christ in him (Gal. 2:20).

If we say that a pagan cannot be forced to live like a Christian by legislation, we must also say that a Christian shouldn't need legislation to convince him to live like a Christian. I can understand a pagan being a racist, a liar, a thief, or lacking compassion for the poor; but I dare not excuse the Christian who does the same thing. If I take Jesus' final commission seriously, I will not only preach and baptize

but also teach and do *all* that He commanded
(Matt. 28:18-20). Luther declared, "If you
preach the gospel in all its aspects with the
exception of the issues which deal specifically
with your time you are not preaching the
gospel at all."

The third mark of a Christlike life, is to be
a *doer of good* (Rom. 12:9-18). Paul makes
it unmistakably clear that while believers are not
saved *by* good works, they are saved *for* good
works (Eph. 2:8-10). Both Peter and Paul
were concerned that Christians be famous for
their love. The apostles warned Christians to
expect trouble with the government. But they
were to make sure that the trouble didn't
result from being troublemakers (Rom. 12:18-21;
1 Peter 4:14-16). Christians were (and are)
to be doers of good—constantly on the offensive against suffering and evil (Rom. 12:21).

Because of this, a Christian never allows his
faith to degenerate into passivism. A case can
be made for Christian *pacifism* but not for
Christian *passivism.* Jesus indicated that bless-
edness belongs to the peace-*makers.* Actively
opposing evil demands a hunger and thirst for
righteousness. At the very least, this demand
prohibits the Christian from being drawn into
a position that passively condones evil.

A fourth characteristic of the Christlike
life demands equal emphasis. The Jesus-follower
is a *submitted* person. A hallmark of the Spirit-
filled person is his attitude of submission to

others (Eph. 5:18-21). This submission is not determined by whether the other person or institution respects that submission or responds to it with appreciation and kindness, but by the believer's ultimate submission to the Lord.

The role of submission is especially crucial with respect to the government. The New Testament's insistence that a Christian obey the law and submit to the government grew out of the knowledge that an attitude of rebellion is contagious. Christians must set an example of respect for law and justice for the sake of peace and order without which the discipling of the nations is virtually impossible (1 Tim. 2:1-2). A Christian is a free man in Christ, but he must be careful to use that freedom in such a way that he does not encourage evil on the part of others (1 Peter 2:16).

Finally, one last Biblical principle must control the Christian response to the God-and-country dilemma––the preeminence of love. The key to Romans 13 is verses 7 and 8, "Pay all of them their dues, taxes to whom taxes are due, revenue to whom revenue is due, respect to whom respect is due, honor to whom honor is due. Owe no one anything, except to love one another; for he who loves his neighbor has fulfilled the law."

A Christian should appreciate and acknowledge the good benefits of even a bad government. Even if believers are persecuted and harassed by evil rulers they are not freed from their responsibility to love.

The preeminence of love requires a Christian to oppose evil at all times. He does not respond to hate with more hate, or violence with more violence. His response demonstrates the radical nature of his commitment to Christ. When Jesus was arrested, Peter drew his sword and attempted to defend his Lord with violence. Jesus stopped him with an emphatic No! That one brief incident should have been enough to disarm the Christian community of its "worldly" weapons forever. The symbol of the faith is a cross, not a sword.

Even when the governmental harassment and opposition to the Christian community became critical, the apostles appealed to the saints, just as Jesus did, to respond to Caesar. The believers were told to honor and obey the officers (Rom. 13:1-5; 1 Peter 2:13-17; Titus 3:1), to pay their taxes as responsible citizens (Rom. 13:6-7) and to faithfully pray for their political leaders (1 Tim. 2:1-2). Those who follow Jesus are called upon to live with the constant tension of life in two worlds. They must learn to respect and submit to Caesar because of their Lord. Yet at the same time they can never forget that Caesar is not and can never be their Lord.

PATRIOTISM AND IDOLARTY

Patriotism goes too far when a person equates love for country with allegiance to God. Some

Christians have made patriotism synonomous with religious zeal—God and country are inseparable concepts, and since "God is on our side" it is justifiable to say, "Our country, right or wrong." This is taken to mean a blanket endorsement of national policies. The danger, however, is that one's patriotism can become idolatry. To put one's nation above God weakens a Christian's true witness in the world.

For Discussion

1. Why does mankind need government? If government itself is instituted by God, can one justifiably resist it? How does the sinfulness of man relate to the need for human government?

2. How do you measure a person's patriotism? Does "flag waving" mean one is patriotic? Is it unpatriotic to disagree with government policies?

3. Must a Christian obey all the laws of his country even if they are contrary to what he conceives of as God's will? Why or why not? When should laws be disobeyed?

4. Is a Christian ever justified in giving unlimited loyalty to his government in the name of patriotism? Why or why not?

5. Is it dangerous to equate "God and country?" Why or why not? In what way is the democracy of the United States different from Israel's theocracy? Why didn't their theocracy assure their survival?

6. Why should Christians avoid assigning degrees of patriotism to political parties or to ideologies such as *liberal* and *conservative?* Can you say one point of view is more patriotic than the other?

7. How far should a Christian go in resisting a wicked or corrupt political regime?

8. How should a Christian show support for his government without conflicting with allegiance and loyalty to God?

9. In a country that asserts that "all men are created equal," is it unpatriotic to allow racism and discrimination against minorities? Why or why not?

7

Can the Church Survive
the State?

*As government supplies more of the needs and
wants of American citizens, it wields more
power. It begins to encroach upon individual lives
and liberties. People are sensitive about their
personal liberties, whether they are threatened
by legislative action or court decisions. Americans have always accepted in principle the doctrine of the separation of church and state. It
is a complex idea that Christians need to face
and evaluate in the light of their religious
freedom and action. Nolan B. Harmon, a retired
bishop of the United Methodist Church, describes a "relation of equity" between church
and state. "Both church and state should face up
to the fact that they never have been, and cannot now be, separated in the life of the ordinary
man to the extent that the framers of the First
Amendment thought possible."*

As the Supreme Court continues to hand
down decisions in the area of church-state separation, it seems that the separation long ac-
claimed as fundamental American policy is more
of a constitutional abstraction than a practical
reality. This development is due not to any juris-
tic wavering on the part of the courts but to the
nature of the two powers involved. Up till the
present, efforts to resolve the relation of church

to state in American life have been based on the assumption that a definite line can be drawn between the two. Yet not only past and present history but also certain decisions of the Supreme Court make clear the impossibility of maintaining Thomas Jefferson's strict "wall of separation" between religion and government in the increasingly complex and coordinated landscape of modern life.

For instance, the Supreme Court held it is unconstitutional for a state to provide financial assistance to parochial schools, even if the aid is applied only to the teaching of secular subjects. But at the same time the Court declared in a parallel decision that it is constitutional to finance the construction of facilities at a parochial school as long as the facilities are not used for worship or religious instruction. Previously the Court declared it constitutional for a state to provide money for children's lunches at private schools, as well as to furnish public bus money to take pupils to parochial schools. Although these unusual rights are given to children in parochial schools, a child in a public school may not on school property meet with any minister or rabbi for a bit of religious instruction— that has been declared unconstitutional!

PRAYER IN SCHOOL

One of the most controversial issues in the United States has been prayer in public schools. In many areas school officials have defied the courts and have allowed students to participate in voluntary prayers. Somehow this issue has taken on significance far beyond its importance. Some believe that denying prayer within a school building is a denial of religion and God. However, there has not been an upsurge of conversion to atheism as a direct result of court actions denying public school praying. In many cases where courts overruled the reading of specific prayers, the prayers were so vague few evangelicals would accept their validity anyway.

As someone has suggested, the wall of separation that Thomas Jefferson insisted should be erected between church and state is becoming more and more a serpentine wall, like the *S*-curved brick walls that Jefferson put on the University of Virginia campus. The increasing difficulty of drawing a firm line between the things that are Caesar's and those that are God's is forcing the Court today to meander along a winding path in these matters.

"Absolute" separationists in both church and state seem to want to overlook the depth of state-church involvement we have. The Constitution recognizes Common Law as the law to be administered in the nation's courts, and that Common Law, which has grown and developed through at least fifteen hundred years of English Christendom, is shot through with all sorts of regulations and processes based directly on the Christian religion. "Christianity is part of the law of the land" ruled Chancellor Kent of New York in *People v. Ruggles* well over a hundred years ago as he sustained a sentence in a case of blasphemy. "We are a Christian nation," declared the Supreme Court not very many years ago, "according to one another the equal right of religious freedom, and acknowledging with reverence the duty of obedience to the will of God."

The First Amendment to the Constitution was intended only for the newly created Congress, and not for the several states creating that Congress. "Congress shall make no law respecting an establishment of religion, nor preventing the free exercise thereof." This forbade a national church but did not touch the state church then existing in Connecticut (which lasted until 1817) or that in Massachusetts (until 1833). It was the adoption of the Fourteenth Amendment after the Civil War—which has not a word to say regarding religion—that gave the Supreme Court, so that Court itself held, the right to put down an "impregnable" wall amid the religio-civic complexities of every state and community.

Nevertheless, wall or no wall, that there is a deep Christian involvement in our nation is made clear in ways often cited: Presidents take the oath of office upon the Bible. "So help me God" is a part of courtroom oaths. God is mentioned in our national anthem and pledge of allegiance. "IN GOD WE TRUST" is stamped on our coins. "Sundays excepted" is a notable phrase in the Constitution. Thanksgiving and Christmas are official holidays. Chaplains are provided at public expense for the Congress, legislatures, armed forces, government prisons, and the like. Attendance at church services is required at the military and naval academies. The Supreme Court is opened with the cry, "God save the United States and this honorable court."

The famous Mormon cases of the 1870s brought from the Supreme Court a crucial decision. The Mormons pleaded that polygamy was a religious tenet with them and that the Constitution of the United States protected everyone in the "free exercise" of his religion. Here was a clear-cut issue upon which the Supreme Court took a clear-cut stand, and a definitely Christian one. It ruled that when religious liberty is pleaded at the bar of a United States Court, the standard of judgment "shall be the standard of accepted Christian conduct," and that religious practices outraging this standard "will be uprooted by the law":

> It was never intended that the first Amendment should be invoked . . . against . . . the punishment of acts inimical to the peace, good order and morals of society. Suppose that one believed that human sacrifices were a necessary part of religious worship, would it be seriously contended that the civil government under which one lived could not prevent a sacrifice? Or if a wife believed it to be her duty to burn herself on the funeral pyre of her dead husband, would it be beyond the power of the civil government to prevent her carrying her be-

lief into practice? . . . Government could exist in name only under such circumstances (*Reynolds v. U.S.,* 98 U.S. 145, 1878).

So stood the general attitude of the courts until there came in 1948 the McCollum case. This had to do with allowing children to attend classes for religious instructions in a school during school hours. Mrs. McCollum, an atheist, said her child was subjected to embarrassment and ridicule because he did not go with the others, and sued to prevent the use of school time and school property for religious instruction. Eventually the Supreme Court upheld her contention. Justice Black, speaking for the majority, said: "The First Amendment has erected a wall between Church and State which must be kept impregnable." And where was the "standard of accepted Christian conduct" decreed by the 1879 court?

Some years later came the decision against allowing prayer in the schools. Many Americans felt that these decisions ran counter to the background and ethos of what had been declared to be a Christian nation. The often-proposed constitutional amendment to allow prayer in schools, while it is opposed by many church and secular groups, did receive a majority of the votes of the House of Representatives—indicating a widespread feeling that relief of some sort is needed.

These later decisions have been epochal not so much in emphasizing the old wall-of-separation theory as in directing where that wall is to be. In my opinion, Christianity has been boxed in by these decisions and atheism allowed to have the whole outdoors. Atheism is a religion itself, powerfully adhered to; and to rule for no-religion in the public schools or in the state at large is to establish antireligion by legal fiat. Neutrality is not possible here. In the attempt to be on neither side, the Court has allied itself with a system of belief that is as firm as Christianity or Judaism, and antithetical to both. Congress may make no law establishing a religion, but the courts may do so, it seems, by establishing no-religion as the formal faith of the nation.

Both church and state should face up to the fact that they never have been, and cannot now be, separated in the life of the ordinary man to the extent that the framers of the First Amendment thought possible. Indeed, the Supreme Court itself in the McCollum case stated: "The First Amendment does not say that in every and all respects there shall be a separation of Church and State." It certainly does not, and those churchmen who say they want a church totally free of government are unrealistic. What of the policeman who guards the church neighborhood, the deed that secures the church property in the courthouse, the laws protecting public worship, the very coins that go into the collection plate—or shall every church be a miniscule Vatican City? Church and state are *not* separate in American life. At a thousand points man's religious loyalty crosses the lines of his social and political destiny. For almost two centuries we have indeed preserved a curious and praiseworthy equilibrium between our governmental and ecclesiastical machinery in the United States, but there has never been a clear-cut separation of the two so that the one had no concern in the affairs of the other.

We must frankly acknowledge that while church and state are and must be *organically* distinct, they are inextricably locked together in a mutual commonweal. There are many instances in life where there are divided loyalties, entangled communal rights, and "conflicts of interests," and to meet such situations Anglo-Saxon jurisprudence long ago worked out a vast system known as *equity*. By its rules and processes, equity endeavors to determine the just rights of the parties involved in each case.

Courts of equity attempt to remedy situations where strict application of the letter of the law would work unfairly. There is sometimes a harshness about the law when it is rigidly applied that our English forebears saw long ago could make for injustice rather than justice. So eventually there arose chancery courts, or courts of equity, with the judge becoming "chancellor" and determining what is fair to both parties.

As an illustration of entangled rights, think of the equity a city has in a public franchise, such as a bus line, waterworks, or airport. These concerns, though privately owned, are "public" utilities. Their operation is of vital concern to the city itself. Just what the equity is in each instance is difficult to determine. When the question is before a chancellor, every aspect of the particular case must be considered.

So it should be in working toward an equitable adjustment between any church or religious group and the American state. The exact amount of interest a nation has in its churches, or in an individual church, is an indeterminate matter, just as is the "interest" a church has in the well-being of its overarching state. The whole relationship is one to be debated in specific application, but not to be denied in its larger implications. The church has an equity in the state and the state has an equity in the church; or, to put it in common parlance, each has a stake in the other.

This equitable viewpoint, while it will determine nothing with finality and will frankly open the way for more "serpentining," will at the same time give a better background for the cooperation that must prevail. Equity would seem to allow those churches that have put the most into the life of the nation to feel they rightly have a greater share in the nation than others. Christianity certainly has a far greater equity in the United States than has atheism, for instance.

And, frankly, unless we can get our courts to rule in equity, I do not see how we can keep the wall of separation from constricting the religious forces of the land more and more.

How, it may be asked, may small minorities and individual rights be protected? Equity is a vigilant champion at precisely that point. "He that would have equity must do equity" is a fundamental maxim. In other words, if you come to plead your cause in a court of equity, your own hands must be clean. Every minority must plead in fairness in order to ask for fairness.

But the majority has its rights. In deciding that when the standards of religious liberty were appealed to, these must be the standards of "accepted Christian conduct," the Supreme Court did no violence to Mormon elders in Utah comparable to what it would have done had it ruled against generations of men and women whose Christian ethics would never permit them to accept polygamy, and who had, moreover, spent their lives carving this nation out of a wilderness.

What future decisions equity may call for in the church-state imbroglio, as ever-increasing complexities arise, cannot be known. I would like to feel, however, that the august justices will decide future cases in a spirit of balanced justice rather than legal rigidity.

For Discussion

1. Why did the doctrine of separation of church and state become necessary in the early years of our republic? Are those conditions or dangers still present?

2. What are some of the dangerous misconceptions about the doctrine of separation of church and state? Does it mean that politicians should never express religious principles in public or in official business?

3. What do the inscriptions on our coins and the references to God on official documents tell us about our founders' conceptions of the doctrine of separation of church and state?

4. What are some of the benefits your church receives from "the state" (local, state, or national laws, etc.)? Should these be withdrawn to assure real church and state separation? Why or why not?

5. If the church accepts government benefits, should it be wary about government regulations? Is there any evidence government wants to control the ideas and financial programs of the church?

6. Should any church activity come under government control? What controls can be considered legitimate? What about churches engaged in secular businesses? Why do people fear government encroachment in these areas?

7. Would you favor taxation of church properties or income? Why or why not? Is it right for pastors to get preferred income tax treatment? Do other professional people get tax breaks? What about businesses?

8. Can you think of any laws that hinder your church's presentation of the gospel? What laws assist your presentation of the gospel? Do such laws discriminate wrongly against others' freedoms?

9. What could become of our liberties if we did not have a strong constitution and democratic form of government? Why is religious liberty usually stifled in a dictatorial state?

8

Why Should Christians Enter Politics?

During the height of the Watergate trials many people believed that the prosecutors were "too hard" on President Nixon and his aides because "all politicians do that same kind of thing." People lost faith in most politicians because of the unethical behavior of a few. While there are very few angels among politicians, there aren't many angels in other professions either. But two wrongs don't make a right. But a few bad apples don't necessarily mean all are rotten, either. There are many leaders in our local and national political life who are truly concerned about integrity and honest leadership. Mark Hatfield, senator from Oregon, spoke of this kind of leadership, and the need for Christians to become involved in the political structures.

We are stunned to hear a subcabinet official state that the government has the right to lie to the people. We hear talk of the "credibility gap" in the government. Scandalous revelations of the misconduct of congressmen and senators remind us of the moral frailty of men. Influence-peddling and fraud by government employees cause us to wonder what has become of integrity in public service.

The standard reaction to all of this by the American public has been to draw a general rule from specific cases and to condemn everyone in public office as a crook. For men who take seriously their moral convictions and Christian faith, there is a grave question as to whether a Christian could enter politics and still keep his faith. Because of this, many good, honest people avoid politics and seek "safer" vocations. This approach creates a serious vacuum of morality in places of public leadership.

While condemning their public officials, most Americans fail to realize that they are pointing their fingers at the "representatives of the people." These men hold office because we, the people, put them there.

Indeed, the government at all levels is no better than the demands of the citizens. If the people pursue excellence they can require it from their public officials. If each of us, as citizens, expects moral and ethical leadership in government, we ought to be prepared to render that kind of service ourselves.

There is an old saying: "All that is necessary for evil to triumph is for good men to do nothing." This is precisely where we find ourselves today in the matter of Christian ethics and political morality. For too many political generations too many good men have done nothing.

Men changed by a confrontation with Christ must build a changed world. Christians must become involved in the processes of transformation in our world, as God leads them. One of the

major processes for orderly change is politics—
the art and science of government.

For the Christian to reason that God does not
want him in politics because there are too many
evil men in government is as insensitive as for a
Christian doctor to turn his back on an epidemic
because there are too many germs.

SICK NEED A DOCTOR

*Not to enter politics because you would have to
associate with some evil people is not the principle Jesus followed. He came and lived in the
midst of evil men. He was criticized for associating with "publicans and sinners." His answer to
His critics was, "Sick people need the doctor,
not healthy ones! I haven't come to tell good
people to repent, but the bad ones" (Mark 2:17,
Living Bible).*

*Jesus knew that the only way to attack infec-
tion was to apply the medicine directly to the sore.
If Christians really want to heal society's wounds,
they will have to touch the patient, as difficult
as that may be. Isolation is not holiness. God
insisted, "Be holy as I am holy," but then He
deliberately entered a defiled world and demonstrated His holiness in Jesus Christ.*

The solution to the problem of immorality
in public office begins with the character of the
people of this nation. It must begin with us. Ask
yourself these questions: "If everyone took the
same interest in government that I do, what kind
of government would we have? If everyone
obeyed the law, including traffic laws, with the
same faithfulness that I do, what kind of crime

rate would we have? If everyone accepted public service or community work with the same attitude that I do, how much would get done for the public good?"

This, then, is the twofold challenge to the Christian citizen. First, to redeem the citizens of our society and thereby to build a better foundation for government. And, second, to be willing to serve God in politics and government if that is where He wants you.

Let us turn now from this discussion of the citizen's responsibility for morality in government to some thoughts about the relationship of a leader's personal spiritual life to his public service. Of course, the need for personal faith is not limited merely to those involved in public service. The trials, temptations, sense of void and loneliness can be present in any person's life, regardless of his profession.

There are certain problems, however, which are perhaps intensified by a political career. Among these is the temptation of the ego. There are tremendous pressures in public service to fixate upon one's own importance. The man who falls in love with his own image loses all touch with real human needs, all perspective on his own capacities. The political leader with an inflated ego makes no room for God in his life and suffers from the blasphemous delusion that he has no such need.

In my own life, I know of no solution except a personal, daily relationship with Jesus Christ.

We die when our lives cease to be daily renewed by the steady radiance of His love.

Another intensified problem for the public servant is that it is easy to forget what it means to serve. True service involves neither condescension nor exploitation. Our call to serve is not because service has been earned, but rather because each man is of divine worth. Christ provides the example: "If I then, your Lord and Teacher, have washed your feet, you also ought to wash one another's feet" (John 13:14).

The personal spiritual life of a man should be his constant source of strength. The need is great. Abraham Lincoln admitted: "I have been driven may times upon my knees by the overwhelming conviction that I had nowhere else to go." A daily relationship with God in prayer helps us not to confuse our will with His.

Any person in public life who thinks that he can "go it alone" is tragically mistaken. No man has enough love, concern, humility, strength, courage. In an individual's friendship with God there comes each day the humility of being forgiven and the strength of being renewed.

Because Christianity is a relationship, not a dogma, it provides a dynamic absolute for one's life. The temptation to lose sight of any absolute is particularly intensified in the political arena. Our democratic system holds that the best political policy is not derived from some political absolute, but formulated through the legal clash of many relative views.

I can accept neither simplistic dogmatism nor total relativity. My relationship with Christ gives me a base both for my personal and public life. This is the one constant factor running through all of life. The dynamics of this relationship give the Christian both an absolute foundation and the freedom to deal with the relativity of the political sphere. There is a perspective, an equilibrium, and a total world view which the Christian can achieve. This gives him the capacity to deal with relative and changing circumstances.

Yet how does this Christian belief affect the mechanics of government? As a public official, I have as much responsibility to the non-Christian as to the Christian. And I firmly support the full separation of church and state. The responsibility of the public servant is not to Christianize the institutions of government, but to bring the influence of Christ to bear on them.

Christ recognized our human tendency toward institutionalism when He forbade Peter from building three monuments on the Mount of Transfiguration. We cannot capture great spiritual truths in concrete or in law. Both statues can become forms of idolatry. And there often is an abdication of our individual responsibility. No amount of government legislation can replace the function of the church which is to change men's hearts by the power of Christ.

CHANGING STRUCTURES IN SOCIETY

Some Christians have confused the mission of the church with the responsibility to influence political structures for good. They go too far in trying to convert institutions in order to influence individual human behavior rather than seeking to convert individuals in order to influence institutions. Perhaps the best Christian strategy is not to reject either option, but to use both ways as a means to spreading the influence of Christ in society.

If the Christian faith is to have an effect on the mechanics of government, it must be through the lives of public officials coming together in God, in the recognition that they need God's guidance and grace in carrying out their public duties. The Christian faith cannot affect the mechanics of government unless it affects the lives of individual men who bear influence on these institutions.

We cannot discuss the subject of Christian ethics and politics without touching briefly on the matter of how men can be faithful Christians and still differ politically.

Our difficulty here comes when we allow ourselves to fall into the idolatry of marrying our particular brand of theology to a certain political philosophy.

LESSONS FROM WATERGATE

In recent years some evangelical leaders "got

burned" because of their close association with the Nixon administration. Watergate taught many evangelicals a lesson that needed to be learned. One's political philosophy should not be fused with his theological beliefs. Christianity is bigger than one political point of view, whether it is conservative or liberal. Sanctifying a political philosophy or a politician inevitably leads to trouble. Maybe that's why Jesus and Paul did not take sides politically, even though their words and manner of life could not help but touch on politically explosive issues.

It is dangerous for us to read into Scripture any particular political point of view. Christ's teachings and the letters of Paul are very clear. We must be willing to be disturbed enough by what we read in the Bible to allow the Spirit of God to change us as individuals so that we may change our world.

We must also recognize the ultimate hand of God in the affairs of men. If two Christians disagree on a political matter, they both could be wrong. They both need to recognize that God is at work in history and that His will is to be accomplished regardless of their political opinions. Our duty is to remain faithful to God above all else and to follow Him as He guides us through prayer, Scripture, and the Holy Spirit.

No matter how we regard the politics of our government, the commandment of Christ and the teaching of Paul indicate clearly that we are to obey the appointed authorities in all points over which they have rightful authority.

Christ admonished His disciples to "render to Caesar the things that are Caesar's, and to God the things that are God's" (Luke 20:25).

Paul exhorted Timothy: "First of all, then, I urge that supplications, prayers, intercessions, and thanksgivings be made for all men, for kings and all who are in high positions, that we may lead a quiet and peaceable life, godly and respectful in every way. This is good, and it is acceptable in the sight of God our Savior" (1 Tim. 2:1-3).

It is much easier for us to criticize our public officials than it is for us to pray for them. Yet this is God's will. This is a practical point of departure from which we can begin to have an influence on our government and its officials. Prayer changes men. Your prayers can change history. Your faithfulness to God as a Christian can mean the difference in the destiny of America.

For Discussion

1. Why do people believe that politics corrupt people? What evidence is there that politics will eventually corrupt a person? Can it just as well be said that "business corrupts" or "sports corrupt?" Why or why not?

2. How can the idea that politics corrupt be changed? What role can Christians play in bringing this change to reality?

3. What is it that *does* corrupt some politicians? How much blame can be put on those who elect and keep corrupt leaders in office?

4. How should people prepare for political careers? What is the best kind of training? Do religious people generally make good politicians? Why or why not?

5. What evidence, if any, is there in Scripture that Christians should avoid political careers? Why didn't Jesus speak more directly to the problems of Rome's relationship to the Jews?

6. How did Joseph view his circumstances as a man of power and political influence (Gen. 45:7-8)? Would this be proper motivation for entering politics or government service today?

7. How did Nehemiah's position as cupbearer to the king of Persia influence the fortunes of his people (Neh. 1–2)? What does his experience tell us about the importance of having political influence?

8. Why wasn't Daniel defiled when he took leadership within a corrupt and pagan empire (Dan. 6:3, 10-24)?

9. Is a Christian politician compromising his faith if he subscribes to the view that he is a servant of "all the people," even those who do not honor God? Explain.

10. What can churches do in a community to influence political leaders to be honest and active in their efforts to seek the common good? Should the church ever become an organized pressure group? Why or why not?

9

How Can Christians Influence Political Decisions?

After fifteen years as a newsman, Robert M. Shaw joined the staff of Senator Warren M. Anderson, majority leader of the New York State Senate. He is publications editor for the Senate Office of Communications, Albany, New York. Mr. Shaw considers the question, "What Are You Doing in Politics?"

Although the word itself does not appear in most translations of the Bible, politics—and political maneuvering—are very much in evidence in both the Old and New Testaments. Much of what the Bible says about those activities is helpful for the Christian in determining his political attitudes and activities today. It can help him in becoming a more responsible Christian citizen, in choosing the right kind of leaders, and in maintaining quality in government.

The approach to politics, at least in the Old Testament, is quite simple. The judges and kings of Israel were put into office by God, and received virtually absolute authority from Him. In those days, the political platform was simple to write. There were no lobbyists to contend with. God's will and the national interest were one and the same thing.

DEFINITIONS

Webster's defines politics *as: 1) the art or science of government; 2) the art or science concerned with guiding or influencing governmental policy; 3) political affairs or business, specifically competition between interest groups or individuals for power and leadership in a government or other group; 4) the total complex of relations between men and society.*

These definitions are in no way contrary to the base of Christianity drawn from both Old Testament law and New Testament love. Such definitions seem binding upon Christians. To reject them would lead to anarchy, for people must be ruled and the quality of government depends upon the character and morality of its political leaders. Politics is people. Christians, of all people, should be interested in the nature and success of the political process.

In some ways, Biblical accounts of politics can be compared with political reporting today in newspapers, magazines, and in network news programs on the radio and TV.

In today's headlines about government leaders —and in the Scriptural accounts of the lives of Israel's rulers—we find details of their flaws, and their misconduct and their indiscretions in both their public and private life.

The misdeeds of Israel's leaders were direct violations of God's commandments as well as violations of the public trust. More importantly, they signified a breakdown in the personal relationship between God and man. But the people of Israel were given a way out when government got out of hand. They could turn to God for relief from an evil or oppressive ruler. In this, some see the seeds of the political revolution that was to manifest itself in the history of our own country.

But there is another side to this. The people of Israel often suffered under an oppressive ruler because of their own evil conduct and their disobedience to God's commandments. We need to remember this when we feel inclined to judge the ethical conduct of political leaders in our own country!

Our modern political philosophy is a legacy not only from Hebrew history but also from the heritage of Greece and Rome. In Athens, for instance, it was customary to publicly examine a candidate's character before he could serve in a public office.

Today, if we are fortunate, we catch a glimpse of a public official's income tax records or, as in one celebrated case, bring out the fact that he once was under treatment for a fairly common emotional problem. In Athens, no facet of the life of a candidate was protected from public scrutiny. The candidate had to prove that he was free from physical defect and free from scandal. He had to show that he had paid his taxes in full, and his military record was held up for review.

Today our schools teach civics and government. Likewise, the education of young men in

Athens included instruction in the responsibilities of citizenship. But that education also emphasized the nobility of public service.

With all that emphasis on qualifications and the virtue of accepting responsibilities, one would think that Athens would have had the finest public officials of all time. But the historian Thucydides says that hardly a man in public life in Athens was free from charges of corruption. And don't forget the legend of Diogenes, walking the streets of the city, his lantern held high in broad daylight, looking for an honest man. This is a bit misleading, I am sure, because other Greeks—especially Aristotle and Plato—made some real contributions to politics and government which are still with us today.

The Romans also made some good contributions, such as the philosophy voiced by Cicero that all men are created equal. Cicero believed that political service was the epitome of human achievement.

Then there was Seneca, the cynic who said that most people were so vicious and corrupt that any form of popular government would be even more evil and oppressive than living under a despot. He figured that a career in politics could offer a good man little except the annihilation of his goodness.

Probably many Americans, both in and out of the church, go along with at least that much of Seneca's philosophy. But Seneca was not a complete cynic. He didn't believe that good and wise men should withdraw completely from public life. He believed, as did Cicero, that every man had a moral obligation to offer his services in one form or another. That may have been the genesis of voluntary private action for the benefit of the community. All of these ideas and systems, and more, have filtered down to us today. We have refined and combined and come up with a political system which draws together—we hope—the best that each culture has to offer.

BALANCING FUTURE WITH NOW

Probably one of the strongest reasons for Christians' withdrawal from political life has been a misinterpretation of Biblical "separation" from the world. Some conservative Christians shun politics because it is "dirty," and they do not want to be corrupted. Others focus their attention on the future—stressing a person's relationship with God and happiness in heaven. But the heaven-oriented Christians overlook attention upon the present and right relationships to men in community. They forget one cannot be properly related to God in heaven without a right relationship to men on earth. You cannot love God without loving men (1 John 4:20). Christians who put down political involvement, who fail to vote or take an interest in community concerns, will not be prepared to face the God who will judge all men. Social and political involvements should be the natural outcome of spiritual transformation. It takes transformed people to transform society.

How well have we done? From a look at the

headlines practically any morning, it's easy to get the impression that the scales are badly out of balance. And the first reaction of most people outside government that I have run into—and that includes some dedicated people in my own church—is to draw a single conclusion: Everybody in public office is a crook.

This creates problems for those of us who take our Christian faith seriously, because we begin to wonder whether a Christian can get into politics and stay there without losing his Christian faith and principles. A lot of good, honest people are avoiding politics or are getting out of politics because of this.

Personally, I had mixed feelings when former Senator Harold Hughes of Iowa decided not to run for another term in the United States Senate so he could go into full-time religious work. I admire him for his decision. We need more men of his dedication and zeal in religious work. But we also need more men of his conviction in our government!

Senator Hughes had been a major voice in Congress on humanitarian issues. But he believed that he followed God's will by getting out of politics to work with two foundations with which he is associated. He hoped he could be as effective outside government as inside. He summed up what he was trying to do this way: "This nation is on the edge of a precipice. The government will not make the decisions that are necessary unless the people set higher standards and demand these decisions."

He says a lot when he says it's up to us. Because when we condemn our public officials for misconduct or for lack of positive action, most of us fail to realize that we are pointing the finger at the men and women who represent us. They are in office because we, the people, put them there. We helped elect them—the good and the bad—either by voting for them or by failing to vote. We have to remember that government at all levels is going to be no better than we, the citizens, demand.

Our founding fathers worked on the basic assumption that democracy would set free the best that is within us. They hoped that this would create the greatest good for the greatest number of people. But they were realistic, too. They recognized that man can be selfish, dishonest, and tyrannical. So they built the government in such a way as to guard against tyranny and to protect the people from selfish governors.

The result is a political system in which the three branches of our government provide a separation of powers and a system of checks and balances—and in which the political parties provide the balance of various interests to arrive at the common good. The political system that we have today recognizes that the public official is the servant of the people and has been entrusted with their delegated powers.

If we are after excellence, then we can require

it from our public officials. If we seek righteousness, then our leaders should point the way. If each of us as citizens expects moral and ethical leadership in government, we ought to be prepared to render that kind of service ourselves whenever we're called upon to do so.

We can begin to see where the solution lies when we ask ourselves these questions posed by Senator Mark Hatfield of Oregon in his book *Conflict and Conscience*:

—If everyone in America were just like me, what kind of country would this be?

—If everyone took the same interest in government that I do, what kind of government would we have?

—If everyone obeyed the law, including the speed limit, with the same faithfulness that I do, what kind of crime rate would we have?

—If everyone accepted public service or community work with the same attitude the I do, how much would get done for the public good?

—If everyone obeyed his conscience and the spiritual commandments of God with the same faithfulness and courage that I do, what kind of world would this be?

THOSE WHO FIT THE MOLD

Some Christians have welded their conservative theology with their conservative politics. They support politicians who fit their own mold, those who are for less federal spending on welfare, but more on military arms. They consistently vote against community improvements which will help those in a lower economic state, and automatically reject government programs that spend money on the disadvantaged. They complain about the evils of welfare but do not refuse government help when disaster hits them.

While many people consider themselves conservative in their religious beliefs they tacitly accept a "civil religion" that amalgamates God into government. It never dawns on them that they might be compromising their understanding of God in the process. They put much emphasis on public prayers, God's name in public documents, prayer in public schools, and other measures which give an aura of religiosity to government.

Yet these same people would not consider having their name on a ballot for public office. To do so might "compromise" their faith. It would take too much of their time from "the Lord's work." They must spend all their time promoting the kingdom of God. So, non-involvement becomes their political attitude. They speak highly of "God and government" but do not participate in the affairs of their own government, local or national. It is not enough to hold sophisticated political ideas if those concepts do not impel you to put those ideas to work. Christians must learn how to "do good unto all men." That may very well mean plunging into the political process.

How do we cope with this temptation to stand aloof from politics? I think the answer lies in the application of the gospel, not only to what we do as members of the church, but to what we do as members of the political system as well. If the message of the gospel applies at all to human relations, then it must surely apply to politics and government. We need change, the kind of change brought about by men who themselves have been changed by the gospel. And then we need involvement, not just observation, by these changed men.

For a Christian to rationalize that God doesn't want him in politics because there are so many corrupt and evil people there makes about as much sense as a doctor saying God doesn't want him to treat an epidemic because there are so many sick people.

The philosopher and economist John Stuart Mill, when writing about representative government, said that if we ask ourselves what it is that good government depends on, we will find that the most important factor is the quality of the society over which the government is exercised.

Senator Hatfield expressed the same idea very well when he wrote:

> The American people have made the kind of government they have today. If there is evil, immorality, and unethical behavior in government, the American people must share in the shame for these conditions. Where there is nobleness, honesty, integrity, and goodness, the American people may take credit for that, too.

Or, in the words of Christ: "The measure you give will be the measure you receive."

The real impact of Christianity on the world of politics and government is not the "official" influence of synods and conferences, of councils and committees. Rather, it is the combined force of individuals who do whatever they do with a full sense of accountability to God and a sense of dedication to the common good.

This influence is exerted as a voter, as a candidate for public office, in filling out your income tax returns, in serving jury duty, in writing to your congressman or to your newspaper, in helping arrange a candidates' forum at election time.

In these and countless other ways, the citizen can witness his Christian principles. By getting involved, the Christian citizen will put his personal integrity to work—not by avoiding politics but by accepting the challenge.

For Discussion

1. Discuss some of the ways a Christian can influence political decisions on a local, state, and national level. How can these be used by members of your church?

2. Does one have to compromise any of his religious beliefs to be involved in governmental activities? to voice opinions? to become involved in political campaigns either for a candidate or for a political issue?

3. Why do so many Christians take no concern about influencing the political processes of our nation? What can be done to excite greater interest in political involvement among Christians?

4. Can the demise of morality in our nation be blamed on Christians' limited interest in practical politics? Why have Christians been weak when it comes to the practical side of politics, in contrast to such groups as Irish Americans, blacks, etc.?

5. If you suddenly got turned on about political involvement, how would you get started? To whom would you go? Would you have a hard time closely associating with non-Christians?

6. How does faith in Christ minister to the welfare of fellow citizens in its practical outreach? Can Christian love be administered through governmental action? How?

7. What is a Christian response to Christian leaders who hold political positions in opposition to oneself? Can one be Christian in his opposition to another's political views?

8. What issue within your community or state would benefit by more Christian involvement in the community? What can you do to become involved yourself or to involve your church?

9. Should a local church give public political support to one of its own members running for political office? If his or her candidacy will improve the moral tone of the community?

10. Should churches become involved in politics only when the lines are clearly drawn between good and evil? When should churches, if at all, become involved in politics? Does tax exemption deter churches from taking a strong moral stand on issues?

10

Do We Still Believe in Liberty and Justice for All?

Christians have a definite motive for entering politics. Not because they want a sense of power or political gain, but because they believe in "liberty and justice for all." They realize the only way that good can be assured is when good men do their best to promote integrity, honesty, and enlightened understanding of the issues we face. Christians believe they bring a dimension into the political process that transcends simply winning elections for one particular political party.

Christians see politics as a means of fulfilling the great goals of the founding fathers. When money begins to corrupt our political process, Christians should step in with their sense of justice. When power begins to corrupt, Christians should step in to help put things back into balance. When corruption runs wild, Christians should get involved with their sense of rightness and fair play.

Robert Linder, a former mayor and a Christian with a strong political consciousness, writes concerning Christians' participation in pursuing political justice. The prophet Micah put it most succinctly when he declared, ". . . and what does the Lord require of you but to do justice, and to love kindness, and to walk humbly with your God" (Mic. 6:8).

The United States is no longer the happy republic of days gone by. When Alexis de Tocqueville visited these shores in 1832 he wrote of American society: "It is a hundred times happier than ours . . . this people is one of the happiest in the world." In his farewell address of 1837, President Andrew Jackson observed: "There has never been thirteen millions of people associated together in one political body who enjoyed so much freedom and happiness as the people of these United States."

But a recent poll conducted by the respected firm of Daniel Yankelvich, Inc., disclosed that one of every three American college students today would rather live someplace other than in the United States. This represents a serious reversal from the early 1960s, as well as the 1830s, and poignantly illustrates the growing frustration and despair.

This outlook affects Christian young people as well. Some have dropped out of the political and social mainstream of American life and joined communes or withdrawn more deeply into the separatist pietism of their Fundamentalist forebears. Many are simply demoralized. They have not dropped out or withdrawn, but they do have serious reservations about whether Christian participation in politics will do any good.

The most frequently asked questions by Christian young people are: If I get involved politically, what effect could I have? Would the little I could do make any difference? Can I as a

Christian have a political identity? Can things be changed for the better if I do participate in politics?

With the exception of two years in the military service and several summers doing construction work, I have spent my entire adult life on the college campus as student and teacher. In addition, I have been active in politics in my state and community which has included service as the mayor of our city. Let me share with you a few insights about American politics.

I believe that Christians stand in a place of unique opportunity in today's troubled world. By this I mean that they not only have a chance to share their faith with frustrated and distressed people, but that they also can be active participants in solving some of the major problems now facing mankind. Christians can help by applying the whole gospel to the entire man. This means returning to the Biblical synthesis of deep personal faith in Christ and genuine concern for other people—the classical tradition of historic Christianity.

Specifically, in the political realm Christians can help bridge the gaps of a polarized society, provide stable leadership during the time of extreme unrest and turmoil, and guide change into constructive rather than destructive channels. The ballot box is the primary means but there are many other ways for Christians to be involved in constructive change, including holding public office.

But the question remains, after all the dust has settled, after the sweat and tears of political participation: Will it make any difference? Will it have been worth it in terms of time, talent, and money; especially Christian time, talent, and money? My answer is a simple but emphatic Yes?

First, Christians can be a resistance to extremes and extremism in national political life. Obviously, there are no specific verses in the Bible that warn Christians to shun the Radical Right and the Radical Left, nor may the radical implications of commitment to Christ be denied.

On the other hand, the essence of the gospel makes it clear that a politically involved Christian must be on the side of humanitarian concerns which reconcile, heal, and establish justice, and against a divisive materialism which is insensitive to human needs. This means that the Christian in politics must not only hold to his convictions but also be "as wise as a serpent and harmless as a dove." It is difficult to see how a genuine follower of Christ can embrace the rhetoric, methods, and goals of the political extremists without degrading the gospel. It is not easy to be a moderate and a peacemaker in American politics today; in fact, to act this way is to be a "radical" in the best sense of that term. Yet men and women of this persuasion are desperately needed if democratic nations are to avoid the kind of extreme polarization that leads to totalitarianism.

Second, the contribution of a single individual often has a greater impact than most people realize, even in modern mass society. The classic example of the potential importance of one person's vote in a democratic election comes from the pages of American history. In 1842, an obscure Indiana farmer named Henry Shoemaker cast a vote breaking a tie between two candidates for the State House of Representatives. In the following year, the man elected by Shoemaker's one vote broke a tie in the voting for one of Indiana's United State senators. (At that time senators were chosen by state legislatures.) The United States senator thus chosen—Edward Hannegan—cast the deciding vote in 1845 which brought Texas into the union and later broke the tie in the senate on the issue of war with Mexico in 1846. Thus, farmer Shoemaker's one vote had a profound effect upon the course of American history.

Although the importance of a single vote or the impact of a single voice may be less dramatic in most instances, still it is vitally important to the working of the democratic process. According to men on the inside, more than once a member of Congress has voted on a particular issue in accordance with a persuasive letter he received expressing a constituent's opinion. My own experiences confirm the great importance of individual letters and opinions at the local level of government. Political scientists estimate that any politically concerned person who uses his influence to commend a candidate to a friend in the course of normal day-to-day contacts can win thirty votes for his man at the polls. The role of the Christian in each of these situations can be enhanced to an even greater degree since he presumably will be working for eminently just causes and high-quality candidates. One person can accomplish much!

Equally as important is the corporate political impact of Christians working with other believers or with other people of a like mind. In this respect, a Christian can plunge headlong into the fray. He can become part of the regular party organization, a voluntary ad hoc campaign committee, or the personal campaign staff of a candidate. He should not be deterred by the prospect of having to cooperate with people who may not be Christians and to identify with their concerns and purposes. After all, this does not necessarily mean that he must conform at all times to the spirit and practices of a political group and abandon his own Christian principles.

Perhaps churches should take a stand on important nonpartisan issues. For example, after reading and discussing Francis Schaeffer's book *Pollution and the Death of Man* a local church may want to write letters to state and federal authorities expressing Christian concern for proper environmental controls. Or a group of churches in a community may visit with the officials of a nearby cattle feedlot or steel mill about possible ways voluntarily to control undesirable pollution. These are examples of responsible corporate Christian social action which could result in a change for the better. Further, in these instances the impact of the group would be much greater and more effective than the influence of a single individual.

Does the form of government under which Christians live make any difference? It most certainly does! In modern times, Christians have existed under totalitarian regimes, absolute monarchies, limited monarchies, democracies, and dictatorships of various sorts. Although none of these governments could separate a man against his will from the love of Christ, the political system still makes a great difference in the implementation of the Great Commission. Moreover, most nondemocratic forms of government bring with them certain disabilities for believers, including political ones.

SOME MINISTER TO KEEP OTHERS FREE

Christians who devote much of their life to developing good politics benefit not only their own government, but also freedom to advance the gospel. The thousands of Christians in full-time religious-related occupations should be grateful for the men and women who forsake the comfort and safety of frequent Christian fellowship for the hard and soul-wearing process of associating with many kinds of people in order to preserve the principles and freedoms that make undisturbed religious activity possible. Perhaps we need more men and women willing to dedicate themselves to this task. We need to give more credit to Christians behind the scenes in the political warfare, who indirectly make it possible for Christians to minister Christ openly.

In these critical days there are forces abroad which could destroy all of the positive things for which America stands, including this nation's great Bill of Rights with its guarantees of religious freedom and "life, liberty, and the pursuit of happiness." There are those extremists who would wipe out the last forty years of progress toward social justice in this country. There are alarming dehumanizing trends in American society which will continue and accelerate unless greater numbers of Christians become more politically aware and active. Democracy is not a perfect form of government, but Christians should think twice before standing idly by and watching it be destroyed.

What happens when Christians allow the forces of evil to triumph in the political life of a nation? Nazi Germany in the past generation offers a prime example of this sort of moral irresponsibility. For the most part, German Christians remained silent and did not speak out against Hitler during the years of his rise to power. Too many were Germans first and Christians second to raise any serious objections. After the Third Reich's totalitarian control apparatus had been extended throughout the land, it was a different story and resistance became much more difficult.

The situation in South Africa and Rhodesia

again points out a problem of Christian inaction and support of the status quo in the case of an inhuman apartheid policy. Much the same can be said for many Protestants in Northern Ireland who have adopted a hard-line stance against full civil rights for the Roman Catholic minority there. And, of course, the record of evangelicals in the United States resisting the movement for racial and social justice and objecting to governmental efforts to combat poverty is hardly one of which socially sensitive Christians can be proud.

Yes, it does make a difference! No, many things will not be changed overnight! Real life is not TV where Kojak or Petrocelli wrap it all up in an hour. Politics and tough political problems require wide-scale involvement and hard work. The point is that the political stakes in the present crisis are enormously high; and Christian involvement is not only desirable, it is imperative. Concerted and sustained Christian effort, both individual and collective, can result in both immediate and long-range changes which will bring glory to God and allow all the world to see what a difference Jesus Christ can make in the way a person values his world and the people in it.

The redemptive gospel of the early church was a world-changing message and addressed itself to the needs of the whole man. In the twentieth century it has too often been narrowed to a world-resisting creed by an embarrassing divorce between personal salvation and social

and political involvement. Sir Frederick Catherwood, a noted English Christian layman, cor-
rectly suggests that a refusal to become involved
in public affairs is a breach of the second great
commandment of Mark 12:31. According to
Catherwood: "To try to improve society is not
worldliness but love. To wash your hands of
society is not love but worldliness."

Perhaps Christ will return tomorrow and end
all of the present frustaration and despair. But
remember that Jesus said that no man knows
the exact hour of His coming (Matt. 24:36), and
until His reappearance we are to keep His commandments as we abide in His love (John 15:10;
1 John 3 and 4). In the meantime politics and
life go on.

Should Christians get involved? Will it make
any difference? How can a person who claims to
love Jesus Christ and to accept Biblical authority
and who lives in a democracy answer these questions in anything except the affirmative?

For Discussion

1. What are some of the trends, even among Christians, that tend to dehumanize people and undo the ad-
vances of social justice in this country? Why are some
Christians attracted to these ideas?

2. What are the dangers of blind acceptance of certain
political ideas? Can Christians support a concept of free
enterprise without compromising their sense of social
justice? How? Or why not?

3. In view of how Hitler took over all political and social
control in the wake of church silence, why is it im-

portant for Christians to react quickly to even the slightest encroachment upon human rights?

4. What are the political implications of the prophet Micah's words to "do justice, and to love kindness, and to walk humbly with your God?"

5. How are the aims of Jesus as expressed in Luke 4:18 in harmony with what a modern Christian engaged in the political arena should be doing? Are any of these aims appropriate political goals? Or are they only religious goals?

6. Why is the task of justice more appropriately a political exercise rather than simply an individual effort? Can we be content with an individual ethic of justice?

7. What is justice in terms of understanding equality under the law? Why is this concept of justice an important concern for Christians?

8. Does "justice for all" mean we should strive to make everyone economically equal? Why or why not? Have any countries who have tried this succeeded?

9. Is democracy a form of government well-suited for establishing justice? How well has the American system of government coped with the problems of injustice in America? Racially? Economically? Politically?

11

Should We Fight for Freedom?

Two chaplains, both members of the Officers Christian Union, with long military careers, present their views on a Christian's involvement in military activity and war. The first is a moderate presentation by army chaplain (Col.) E. H. Ammerman. The second, a more militaristic view, is presented by army chaplain (LTC) Peter S. Lent. A short commentary by the compliers separate their views.

Many Christians in America are faced with serious questions about war and the taking of human life. There is no easy answer. We can never feel easy about the taking of human life, regardless of the circumstances. Yet we should remember that the commandment "Thou shalt not kill" really says, "Thou shalt not commit murder." Neither should we forget that God loves not only us, but also our enemies. We cannot escape the need to search for answers, even though we may never be fully satisfied with any answer concerning the frustrations of war. Basically, there are three Christian approaches to the idea of war.

Participation in war is a citizen's responsibility. Some would even go so far as to say, "My country—right or wrong—still my country." Those who hold this position believe that when one's country is at war, the total responsibility is to obey. If this means engaging in active combat and taking human life, it is their obligation to do so. If force is required to maintain law and order, then the Christian should be willing to use force.

This may mean that nations and other social groups operate on a lower moral level than individuals do. Certainly they operate on a lower level than the more morally advanced members of that group do. But the question arises, "Should an individual lower his standards to that of the group?" And those in this first category would answer, "Yes, if necessary to preserve society."

What about responsibility for the deeds committed during war? Can the individual, in good conscience, shift the responsibility for his decisions to his country? After all, in a democracy the weight of responsibility must ultimately come back to rest upon the individual citizens. We are still left with the plaguing question of how there can be any lifting of the moral level of a nation if all its citizens subordinate their individual conscience to the dictates of the state.

Participation in war is only the lesser of two evils. While we live in an evil world, many of our choices will not be between an unmixed good on one hand and unmixed evil on the other. Many decisions will be in the gray area. This may mean that the best choice possible will be the one that involves the maximum of good and the minimum of evil. Persons in this second category concerning war maintain it will always belong in the gray area.

War may be considered inevitable because of the nature of man and his will to power; or because of the dominance of sin in human society; or again, because of the nature of the state as an instrument of power. Perhaps we cannot eliminate war, at least not in our present level of civilization. No doubt there are some nations and people who will not settle their differences except by the use of force. This means any nation that refuses to fight would simply be overrun or liquidated.

The implication is that the lesser-of-two-evils approach should be considered temporary. It is an approach that we must use now, but we should look for a time when we can do better.

Now, the way of Christ is the way of love — yes, even absolute love. But if love cannot be applied at present in all cases, then *equal justice is the next alternative.* Force will of necessity have to be applied to effect justice. And when force is applied on such a large scale as in war, then innocent persons will be hurt. Or would it be pertinent here to ask the question, "Who is innocent, and who not innocent?"

We might ask the question, "Would our president commit murder?" The obvious answer is No. But on the other hand, would he, as commander-in-chief of the armed forces, order men into battle where they will certainly kill and be killed? *Yes!* Here, then, we see one of the meanings of original sin, when we in carrying out the responsibilities of our office must do that which apart from this official reason would be absolutely wrong.

War is wrong and participation in war is wrong. Persons taking this view are called pacifists, or conscientious objectors. There are many degrees of pacifism, and many motives for conscientious objection to war. There can hardly be a description of a typical conscientious objector. We are sometimes a bit suspicious that one may be only trying to avoid responsibility, or may even be a coward.

Some would stop just short of taking human life. Others object to any participation, even in an indirect way, such as paying taxes, or even any productive labor in the nation that is in a war. These last mentioned are the "absolutists," "the idealists," "the perfectionists." But is not *pacifism of the last category indeed anarchy?*

There are others who would say that participation in war is wrong, but who would fall in between the absolutist and the one who would stop just short of taking of human life. He might thus serve as a medic, or in some administrative or support role of the military.

A classic pacifist was Mahatma Gandhi of India. He won his objectives. But let us not forget that he was dealing with Great Britain, a nation that was formed on Christian principles. Our enemies today are not Christian nations.

"If anyone . . . take your coat, let him have your cloak as well" (Matt. 5:40) is used by pacifists. But if you are with your wife and sister and men grab your wife, assault and rape her, would you give them your sister also?

Let us remember that there is no completely right way to take human life. God is the giver of life, and He should be the one to decide when it is called back to Himself, the Giver. We must live with ourselves, and this means that we will differ with some of those around us. Let us have charity in this, and remember that we should love those of our own land who may differ with us on war, even as we are to love our enemies.

WAR—RIGHT OR WRONG

Christians seem to face a dilemma. They are against war and killing but they would be less than honorable to their fellow citizens if they allowed an aggressor to take their land and rape their resources. Perhaps there is no right or wrong answer. Maybe the answer is somewhere in the middle. Why we commit ourselves to fight a war seems to be the vital question. If it is to defend ourselves and our loved ones—then it can be justified. If it is to gain power, riches, or political control at the expense of other human beings it is definitely wrong.

Now read Chaplain Lent's views:

There are many very honest and very devout

Christian pacifists for whom I have great respect. And I believe that as we seek God's will on this issue, we must be open and honest and receptive to His leading. Let us "speak the truth in love." One of the things that disturbs me about some of the people in the "peace" movement is that they speak with so much hostility.

The most common cry of the pacifist is the sixth commandment, which in the King James version reads, "Thou shalt not kill" (Exod. 20:13). In the New English Bible and in most of the modern versions this commandment is translated, "You shall not commit murder," which is what the original means. Remember, the same God who gave the law on Mount Sinai, also led the children of Israel into and through the military conquest of Palestine in which thousands of people were killed. The commandment speaks of premeditated murder, not a military action, and a reading of the remainder of the Law of Moses makes this very clear.

There is no pacifism in the Old Testament. The great heroes of the faith were soldiers. Abraham was not a soldier in the conventional sense, but when a fight came he always left the battlefield victorious. Moses, the great liberator of his people, organized and led the children of Israel in a military fashion. Joshua was the general whose faith, military leadership, and tactics brought victory to Israel in the conquest of Canaan. The great hero of the Jewish nation was the soldier-king, David. Remember what the people chanted about David? "Saul has slain his thousands, and David his ten thousands" (1 Sam. 21:11).

The honest pacifist must go to the New Testament in search of Biblical support for his views. Specifically he must go to the Sermon on the Mount in Matthew chapters 5–7. The two verses that are most important are Matthew 5:39, "But I say to you, do not resist one who is evil. But if anyone strikes you on the right cheek, turn to him the other also," and Matthew 5:44, "But I say to you, Love your enemies and pray for those who persecute you."

These are the words of Jesus, but to get them into perspective we must recognize them as kingdom-of-God principles that relate to personal relationships and action, just as the Ten Commandments relate to personal relationships. The Sermon on the Mount is a statement of the principles of the kingdom of God. To see how Jesus applied them in both kingdom-of-God as well as kingdom-of-this-world situations, we have to consider His words and actions. It's never safe or right to lift one or two verses out of context and use them as proof texts to prove a particular point.

I think that it is instructive, first of all, to get a feel for the New Testament attitude toward the military man. The conversation between Jesus and the Roman centurion (Matt. 8:5-13) is helpful because it lets us hear Jesus speak to a professional soldier. This man was a senior non-

145

commissioned officer who commanded a unit of one hundred men. He was an experienced, dedicated man who had proven himself as a soldier and as a combat leader. He was a highly respected career soldier who talked to Jesus in soldier's language: "Lord, I am not worthy to have you come under my roof; but only say the word and my servant will be healed. For I am a man under authority, with soldiers under me; and I say to one, 'Go' and he goes and to another 'Come,' and he comes, and to my slave 'do this' and he does it" (Matt. 8:8-9). Here is a man who is sure that Jesus has complete authority in the spiritual realm, just as a centurion does over the men in his unit. It is of this soldier that Jesus says, "Not even in Israel have I found such faith" (Matt. 8:10).

There is another centurion mentioned in the New Testament, also a man of faith. His name was Cornelius. He is particularly significant because he was the first recorded Gentile to become a Christian. The story is told in some detail in Acts 10. The household of Cornelius in Caesarea received the Holy Spirit just like the disciples did on the day of Pentecost in Jerusalem. Peter and the other Jewish Christians were astounded that this happened, not because Cornelius was a soldier, but because he was a Roman, a Gentile. So the first non-Jew to become a Christian was a military man, a soldier.

You can also get a feeling of the attitude of the New Testament toward military men by the way military terms are used. In writing to Timothy, whom he considered his son in the faith, Paul exhorts him to "endure hardness as a good soldier of Jesus Christ" (2 Tim. 2:3, KJV). In writing to the church at Ephesus Paul tells them to put on the whole armor of God and then proceeds to use the armor and the weapons of the Roman soldier to illustrate the armor and the weapons of the Christian soldier in spiritual warfare: the helmet of salvation, the shield of faith, the breastplate of righteousness, and the sword of the Spirit (Eph. 6:10-17).

Neither the Old Testament nor the New Testament presents an antimilitary, pacifist position. The profession of arms is honored in both, and the term "Christian soldier" is a Biblical term.

The good Samaritan found the man on the Jericho road robbed, beaten, and left for dead *after* the crime had taken place. What would he have done had he arrived on the scene *while* the crime was being committed? Would he in love and nonviolence have passed by on the other side of the road? What would a group of good Samaritans have done had they arrived on the scene of the robbery in progress? Would they have stood around and bemoaned the violence and waited to see if the man would be dead or alive when it was all over? I think not. But let's take it a step further, what would Jesus and His band of young men have done if they had happened upon this robbery scene in progress on the Jericho road? The point is this: Jesus used physical force in a kingdom-of-this-world situation when He drove the money changers out of the temple. He could not stand by and see poor people exploited by the money changers and sellers of animal sacrifices. So this big, sun-tanned carpenter from Nazareth picked up a stick and drove them out of the temple.

So what would He do if He encountered a robbery on the Jericho road? All the witness of Christ in me says He would go to the aid of the man and do what was necessary to stop the crime. He would first use all the moral force possible, but if necessary he would use physical force as well. I cannot see Him standing by and waiting to see if the robbers killed the man or not, and I cannot see Him directing you or me to act that way either. The task of love is always to aid the one who is being victimized.

This is the role of the peacekeeping force in our society, whether it be a military force or a police force. Both military and police force can be misused and both have been misused, and I suspect both will be misused in the future. There are always some who will misuse the powers entrusted to them. But this is all the more reason why we need Christian men of compassion and unquestioned integrity as military leaders.

It is an honorable thing to be a soldier. It is a great honor to be a Christian soldier, and be aware that we need not only physical arms, but also spiritual armament: the helmet of salvation, the shield of faith, the breastplate of righteousness, and the sword of the Spirit.

For Discussion

1. Do you agree with the assertion that neither the Old Testament nor the New Testament present an anti-military, pacifist position? Upon what Biblical principles or verses would the pacifist rely?

2. Is self-defense and defense of one's family proper Christian grounds for using violence? If yes, how does this affect one's attitude toward the use of arms and toward involvement in the military?

3. How should Christians view supplying military aid to other countries? Is there a difference in sending aid to one country and not another?

4. Would Christian love change our military stance as a nation? How? Would it be feasible on a national level? Could it be brought about?

5. In the face of so may desperate human needs around the world, can Christians justify and support our country's enormous military expenditures? Why or why not?

6. What would happen if more military funds were channeled into humanitarian efforts? Should the Christian lobby for such effort? If so, how?

7. Does the fact of a voluntary army alter the Christian's stance toward war and military service? Consider this in the light of both the pacifist and the militarist views.

8. Should Christians work for peace among nations, or only concern themselves with "spiritual" problems? What can Christian political leadership do to prevent war?

9. If Jesus and His disciples confronted the thief beating the man on the Jericho road, do you think they would have used force against him? Would it have been justified? Why did Jesus speak against Peter's use of force in the garden?

10. Can we use the fightings recorded in the Old Testament as examples of God's approval of war? Why or why not? How can we justify Israel's violence toward her enemies? Does Jesus' teaching alter the Biblical concept of violence and war? How?

12

Is God Going to Judge America?

Nations come and go. The history of the world shows us that no people or nation is safe from destruction. Oswald Spengler and Arnold Toynbee concluded that the rise and fall of nations is cyclical. The Bible presents a similar picture of nations (Dan. 2:20-24, 36-45). In times of world stress like we are going through, people are asking about the future of the United States. Will America last? Can the most powerful nation that existed in the history of the world be destroyed?

Christians of every theological and eschatological persuasion attempt to answer these questions. Often their conclusions are contradictory. Those with premillennarian views seem to have more specific answers. Whether they are the final answers will be judged only by history and the divine Judge.

S. Maxwell Coder discusses the intriguing question as to whether the United States is mentioned in prophecy. According to Coder's strict dispensational view it is . . . because the United States is part of all nations that are mentioned in Biblical prophecies. This viewpoint is not presented as the last word, but as a springboard for your discussion. Regardless of eschatological stance, Christians are in general agreement that any nation that rejects God's sovereignty soon comes under His judgment.

The United States is not mentioned in the Bible. Attempts have been made to identify it under some other name in prophecy, but these efforts have not been proven. It has also been suggested that the omission of any specific reference to America may mean that the nation will not be in existence in the last days. However, the Bible does supply a picture of the United States as it will be just before the second coming of Christ to the earth. (Even if the nation should disappear before He comes, its people would presumably still exist.)

Biblical prophecy deals with the future of "all the kingdoms of the world, which are on the face of the earth" (Jer. 25:26). The Bible contains at least sixty references to *all* nations in the last days, as well as many passages referring to all mankind. It is evident that any prophecy which speaks of *all* nations speaks of the United States and any other country in existence in the end time. We must look at these Scriptures, rather than at a few doubtful texts, for whatever God may have been pleased to reveal about the destiny of our own country or people.

Some nations may disappear from the earth before the Lord comes; others may come into existence. However, if the end of the present order is at hand, as many believe, then we may put the name of the United States of America in passages dealing with all nations in the last days, just as any individual may put his name in place of the word "whosoever" in gospel texts. Prophetic teaching implies that several things will happen to America in the future.

America will lose all of its Christians. This event will be followed by an unprecedented outbreak of violence. The next announced event in God's plan of the ages is to be the supernatural removal of all living believers from the earth (1 Thess. 4:17). When that moment comes and America loses every one of its Christians, a national calamity will have begun. The people of God are found in every area of life. They form the temple of the Holy Spirit (1 Cor. 3:16). Because of their presence, evil is restrained by the Spirit, but this will cease when believers meet the Lord in the air. Since the Holy Spirit is to abide with them forever (John 14:16), He will accompany them when they are taken to heaven. Many believe the end of the Spirit's present restraint upon evil is mentioned in 2 Thessalonians 2:7 (ASV): "There is one that restraineth now, until he be taken out of the way." At that time violence and wickedness will fill the earth as it did in the days of Noah and Lot (Luke 17:26-30).

A SOON SECOND COMING?

The United States is only two hundred years old. Compared to many other civilizations that existed for much longer periods that is young for a nation. Since the first coming of Christ many nations have arisen and fallen and have been forgotten. It is possible that the United States, as a nation, could disappear before the second coming of Christ. The geographical boundaries of what we now know as the United States of America could be called by another name. Strictly speaking, maybe it would be safer to say that there will be a nation or nations occupying the geographical position of the United States, and that (those) nation(s) shall face the judgment of Christ at His coming. Historically speaking, Coder's thesis depends on the relatively soon second coming of Christ.

Democracy will die and a foreign dictator will assume control. A little-recognized ministry of the church will come to an end when the world loses all of its believers. During the present age "supplications, prayers, intercessions, and giving of thanks" have been offered by Christians everywhere for all who are in authority (1 Tim. 2:1-2). No one can appreciate how greatly nations have benefited from the prayers of Christians, nor how dreadful the result will be when this divinely commanded intercession ceases. Distress and perplexity will overtake this country and all others (Luke 21:25). At that time the nations will drink the wine cup of God's fury.

With national leadership reaching the point of madness, the time will be ripe for a dictator to assume control. This great leader is to be given power over all kindreds, tongues, and nations (Rev. 13:7). Democracy will be unable to survive the crisis in the United States, which will be among the nations yielding allegiance to Satan's ruler, the beast.

A remarkable spiritual awakening will sweep the country. As the world enters the darkest days of its long history, God will again intervene on behalf of lost humanity. After war, famine, pestilence, and death have taken their toll, people from the tribes of Israel are set apart and sealed as the servants of God (Rev. 7:4-8). They will preach in all the world the good news that God is about to establish His kingdom (Matt. 24:14). Immediately we read of "a great multitude, which no man could number, of all nations, and kindreds, and people, and tongues" who come out of the great tribulation of those days, cleansed in the blood of the Lamb (Rev. 7:9, 14). A remarkable spiritual awakening is therefore going to sweep over the world.

Pestilence and other catastrophes will greatly reduce the population. As these earthshaking events are taking place, the population will be terribly reduced. Christ described the period as a time of "great tribulation, such as was not since the beginning of the world to this time, no, nor ever shall be" (Matt. 24:21). War, famine, pestilence, and earthquake will terrify mankind.

During this period America will lose all of its Jews as God fulfills His promise, "I will take you from among the nations, and gather you out of all the countries, and will bring you into your own land" (Ezek. 36:24, ASV). The effect of this departure on the nation's economic and cultural life can hardly be imagined.

American armies will suffer a disastrous defeat in a world war centering in the Near East. Since the world dicator is to be empowered by the devil himself (Rev. 13:1-8), it is not surprising to read that in these days the spirits of demons will gather all nations together "for battle on that great day of God Almighty" at Armageddon, a great valley in Palestine (Rev. 16:13-16). Demon influence has always been at work behind America and other nations (Dan. 10:13-20). When "the kings of the earth and of the whole world" invade Palestine, the hand of our sovereign God will also be in evidence. He has said, "I will gather all nations against Jerusalem to battle" (Zech. 14:2). At the height of the conflict, the Lord Jesus Christ will come forth from heaven to smite the assembled nations and defeat their armies (Rev. 19:11-21). American forces will share in this stunning defeat.

WHO KNOWS THE EXACT END?

How sure can we be of our historical perspective? Is it not possible that the United States could be destroyed before the second coming of Christ? Did not many associate the fall of Rome with the end of the world and the second coming? Even in recent history we have witnessed the rise and fall of nations. The Third Reich was to last a thousand years. All events of World War II could have been seen as portents of the end of the world. The extermination of the Jews, the destruction of millions of people, the judgment of nations—yet we now see it only as a foretaste of what the end of the world could be. We can believe that the events as described in the Bible will take place, but perhaps we should refrain from interpreting them so that they have to happen in the imminent future.

All unrighteous Americans will be taken away by divine judgment. Following the crushing of the armies, prophecy describes a kingdom on earth which is to last for a thousand years, with Christ as world ruler (Rev. 20:4-6). This is the promised kingdom for which men have been longing over the centuries. It is to begin with a scene of judgment involving every nation, described in Matthew 25:31-46. "When the Son of man comes in his glory, and all the angels with him, then will he sit on his glorious throne. Before him will be gathered all nations and he will separate them one from another as a shepherd separates the sheep from the goats" (vv. 31-32).

This does not teach that America, as a nation, will stand before a throne of judgment. The Greek word here rendered "nations" is better translated "Gentiles." A judgment of individuals is in view, and it evidently takes place in Palestine (Joel 3:2). The returning King dismisses all unrighteous persons from His presence. The righteous are invited to enter the kingdom. Elsewhere in the world a similar separation takes place. People on farms and in industry (Matt. 24:40-41) and in homes everywhere (Luke 17:34) are taken away in judgment if they are found unrighteous, while the righteous are left to have their part in the kingdom (Matt 24:44-51) as they join "every one that survives of all

the nations that have come against Jerusalem"
(Zech. 14:16).

The United States will have a part in the king-
dom of God on earth and in the eternal kingdom
which succeeds it. For one thousand years this
company of the people of God will take part in
the glorious earthly kingdom of the Lord Jesus
Christ, and Americans will certainly be among
them. After the thousand years are ended the
final judgment of the great white throne will
take place, and the eternal state will begin with
the creation of a new heaven and a new earth
(Rev. 20:6–21:1).

The closing chapters of Revelation carry on
the story into eternity. "The nations of them
which are saved shall walk in the light" of the
new Jerusalem, which comes down out of heav-
en from God (Rev. 21:24, KJV). We are told
that "the kings of the earth do bring their glory
and honour into it [the heavenly city]." This
seems to imply that rule by kings rather than
some other form of government will characterize
eternity. The glory and honor of the nations will
be brought into the heavenly Jerusalem (Rev.
21:24,26).

Here, then, are passages of Scripture bearing
on the destiny of the United States. The final
word is found in Isaiah 9:7 where it is written of
Christ, the governor of the nations (Ps. 22:28),
that "of the increase of his government and of
peace there will be no end." This important
verse suggests that the day is coming when other

parts of the universe may be populated as the everlasting kingdom of God continues to expand in the eternal ages.

AMERICA NOT A CHRISTIAN NATION

Perhaps it is important for us to remember that we are not immune from the judgments of God. America is not a Christian nation and, therefore, free from God's judgments. On the contrary, America is full of murderers, rapists, drunkards, immorality, demon-worship, bestiality, and sex-perversions of all sorts. The question is not whether God will judge America; the real question is when.

Surely we can love our nation and want to see it survive, but we should be realistic about what is going on in America. While we are sitting in our cozy homes and comfortable churches, America is going to hell. But too many Christians are not seeing it that way, and are doing little to defeat the forces of evil that are assuring its demise.

For Discussion

1. Why does God judge nations? What nations has He already judged? How do we know? How did He judge Israel? Why are nations with a greater knowledge of God more likely to face His judgments?

2. Is America ripe for God's judgment? Is there any evidence that God may be judging America already? How can God's judgment be forestalled?

3. Is judgment inevitable because we are in the "last days?" Can we assume that the United States will escape tribulation or judgment?

4. If God judges America, does it have to be related to the "end times"? Would God's judgment on America necessarily mean Christ was coming soon? Why or why not?

5. Will God judge America on the basis of how it has treated the Jews? What has happened to other nations who have mistreated the Jews? What Biblical illustrations are there?

6. Does loss of its religious heritage make America liable to God's judgment? How?

7. Can the presence of millions of Christians in America prevent God's judgment from coming upon it? Why or why not?

8. Does 2 Chronicles 7:14 promise that God's judgment can be averted? How can Christians help bring about revival in America? How successful would revival have to be to withhold God's judgment?

9. If we are in the last days and God's judgment is sure, what reasons are there for trying to bring revival to America?

10. What priorities should Christians give to the question of God's judgment on America? Should they view it from the standpoint of America's place in prophecy, or in relationship to the moral and spiritual conditions that need to be changed?